COLUMBIA UNIVERSITY
STUDIES IN THE
SOCIAL SCIENCES

73

The Series was formerly known as
Studies in History, Economics and Public Law.

THE UNITED STATES STEEL CORPORATION

A Study of the Growth and Influence of Combination
in the Iron and Steel Industry

AMS PRESS
NEW YORK

THE UNITED STATES STEEL CORPORATION

A Study of the Growth and Influence of Combination
in the Iron and Steel Industry

BY

ABRAHAM BERGLUND

AMS PRESS
NEW YORK

The Library of Congress cataloged this title as follows:

Berglund, Abraham, 1875-1942.
  The United States Steel Corporation; a
study of the growth and influence of
combination in the iron and steel industry.
[1st AMS ed.] New York, AMS Press [1968]
  179 p. 23 cm. (Columbia University studies
in the social sciences, 73)
  Originally presented as the author's
thesis, Columbia. Reprint of the 1907 ed.
Includes bibliographical references.
  1. United States Steel Corporation.   I.
Series: Columbia studies in the social
sciences, 73.
HD9519.U6   B5   1968   72-76677
                        338.7/66/910973
ISBN 0-404-51073-6

Reprinted from the edition of 1907, New York.
First AMS edition published in 1979.

Manufactured in the United States of America.

AMS PRESS INC.
NEW YORK, N.Y.

PREFACE

THE following dissertation is an attempt to discuss the rise, character, and influence of the United States Steel Corporation. So much has been written about this organization that little can be said of its history that is absolutely new. The works which have treated this subject, however, have generally been either descriptive rather than analytical in nature, or confined to certain limited phases of its development and financial policies. The purpose of this essay is not so much to give a detailed description of the Steel Corporation as to discuss the influences which gave it birth, and to interpret its general character and reaction upon industrial conditions in the light of those influences. The sources upon which the writer has mainly relied have been the annual reports and other publications of the Steel Corporation itself; several trade journals, of which the most important are the *Iron Age* and *Commercial and Financial Chronicle;* and certain governmental documents, particularly the *Report of the Industrial Commission.* The writer has also derived aid from interviews with officials connected with the Steel Corporation and other steel companies. He is also under obligations to Drs. E. R. A. Seligman and H. R. Seager who have looked over his manuscript and offered several valuable suggestions.

A. B.

MANLIUS, NEW YORK, APRIL, 1907.

CONTENTS

CHAPTER I

INTRODUCTION

CHAPTER II

DETERMINING FACTORS IN THE IRON AND STEEL SITUATION

CHAPTER III

THE BEGINNINGS OF THE STEEL CORPORATION

CHAPTER IV

THE UNITED STATES STEEL CORPORATION

CHAPTER V

THE CAPITALIZATION OF THE STEEL CORPORATION

CHAPTER VI

THE STEEL CORPORATION AND PRICES

CHAPTER VII

MONOPOLY AND IRON ASSOCIATIONS

CHAPTER I

INTRODUCTION

§ 1. The making of iron and steel has probably advanced farther along the line of capitalistic development than has any other manufacturing industry. It has had a large share of the attention of trust promoters; and it is doubtful if any other industry better exemplifies the general character and operations of the so-called trust movement. The conditions which have contributed toward consolidation in iron and steel manufacture have in many respects been similar to those which have facilitated the formation of combinations in general; and the reactions of consolidation upon the conditions contributing toward this movement illustrate some of the most salient tendencies inherent in large-scale production.

The concentration of production which had been going on in the iron and steel industry during the closing decades of the nineteenth century—and especially during the closing years of that century—reached a climax in the formation of the United States Steel Corporation in 1901. The forces or conditions which evolved this organization cannot be stated in a few categorical sentences; nor can their influence be properly gauged by mere statement. In the development of this great consolidation several forces, immediate and remote, industrial and financial, co-operated. Some of these, though usual accompaniments of the evolution of large-scale production, have exercised only subordinate influence; others stand out prominently as determin-

ing factors in the iron and steel situation.   It is with reference to these latter forces or conditions that the existence,
character, and influence of the Steel Corporation can be
best interpreted.

§ 2. Fundamentally, the conditions which gave birth to
this great combination are similar to those which have
given rise to other consolidations.   In several character-
istics, iron and steel goods resemble those which are ordinarily produced under trust management.   They are subject
to standardization—to certain uniformities of shape, size
and quality.   They are in general demand over a wide extent of territory.   They are most economically manufactured on a large scale.   At distances from certain local
points, or places of manufacture, freight charges enter
largely into their prices; and in so far as large producers
have been able to secure better terms in the matter of transportation than their smaller rivals, the movement toward
concentration has been accelerated.

In certain particulars external to the mere manufacture
of iron and steel, the industrial situation has been influenced
by conditions similar to those contributing to the growth
of other combinations.   Intensity of competition, due
partly to mal-adjustments between the number and size of
competing producers and the strength and extent of the demand for goods, have furthered the desire for consolidation.
The protective tariff, too, by limiting the area of competition has encouraged producers to combine in the hope of
securing control over certain branches of the trade in the
home market.   The geographical distribution of the sources
of raw material, in so far as these sources are conveniently
located for a single corporate or unified control, has helped
to the same end.

These influences and others which might be mentioned,
are not peculiar to the iron and steel industry.   The condi-

tions, however, which exercised the most determining effects were peculiar in magnitude and mode of operation. Such were the influences exerted by the existence and geographical distribution within the country of large ore and coal fields; by the superior efficiency of large over small capital; by the extreme fluctuations in the demand for iron and steel goods; and by the restrictions imposed on foreign trade by the protective tariff. All these influences co-operate in promoting the growth of concentration.

As is well known, the existence of the iron and steel industry on any large scale is dependent upon adequate ore and coal supplies and facilities for the easy assembling of material. With these essentials the United States is richly endowed, and it is to-day leading the world in the production of iron and steel. The greater part of this industry is carried on in the northeastern part of the country where the leading producers depend, for their raw material, upon the Lake Superior ore districts and the Pennsylvania and West Virginia coking-coal areas. About eighty per cent of the country's iron and steel is produced from ores mined in the region about Lake Superior. The localization of so much ore within such a limited area with cheap transportation over the Lakes to Ohio and Pennsylvania has favored combination. Dependence upon the same or adjacent sources of raw material, common transportation facilities, and trade in the same market have brought producers into relations with one another which have not infrequently led to pooling or consolidation of interests. Geographical conditions, therefore, have favored the growth of the industry in the United States, and have facilitated to a very appreciable extent the tendency toward concentration.

More potent even than geographical conditions in developing this tendency has been the superior efficiency of large capital. There are other industries which require a great outlay of capital for the most economical production, but the making of iron and steel is in a pre-eminent sense the industry of large capital. The proper equipment of a steel plant for effective competition involves extraordinary costs. Not only must the rolling mills be furnished with elaborate and adequate machinery, but the producer must be prepared to manufacture his own iron and steel, and even secure his own ore and coal fields. Such a condition is incompatible with mere individual or partnership management. It necessitates not only corporate control, but involves a consolidation of interests engaged in different stages of production. The nature of the industry itself thus tends toward large-scale production; and this helps to limit its management and control to a relatively small number of producers.

Co-operating with these influences making for concentration there have been violent oscillations in the demand for iron and steel due to alternating periods of prosperity and depression. No other industry is more susceptible to general trade conditions or has been more influenced by such susceptibility. The fluctuations which have characterized the iron and steel industry explain much of the tendency toward consolidation and in no small degree the special character which consolidations have assumed. The demand for iron and steel is great or small according as the times are prosperous or dull. The opening up and shutting down of furnaces and mills, incident to this changing demand, involve much waste; and hence the necessary cost of production is greater than if the demand for goods were normal and steady. During a prosperous epoch, also, an unduly large number of producers are induced to enter the industry; and this makes competition exceedingly severe and even ruinous during a period of depression. These considerations make some control over the conditions of the trade peculiarly desirable from the standpoint of producers.

Furthermore, this varying demand for iron and steel has influenced the character of the resulting consolidations. It was the stress of competition during dull times that led the manufacturers of finished material to reduce as far as possible their costs by securing the sources of their raw material and the producers of crude material to extend their markets by manufacturing finished goods. This tendency has resulted in making the more important combinations largely independent and self-sufficient—a feature which is pre-eminently characteristic of the industry. Capitalization has also been influenced by these oscillations. Combinations, as a rule, are formed during periods of prosperity or rising prices. Capitalization is generally based upon real or supposed earning power. As earnings are more than normal during so-called brisk times, capitalization tends to become inflated. It is true that monopoly advantages resulting from consolidations have been capitalized; but the fluctuating character of the iron and steel trade must be looked upon as a prime cause of what has been considered the over-capitalization of the Steel Corporation and its constituent companies.

The influence of the tariff has been not unlike that in other industries. In restricting foreign competition it has rendered control of the industry within the country easier of attainment. As great consolidations are usually formed with the object of controlling trade, the existence of the tariff has been an important factor in fostering their growth. Such combinations as the American Tin Plate Company and the American Steel and Wire Company, whose aims were monopoly control, would hardly have been formed without tariff protection. These companies included practically all the plants of the country in their respective lines, and were enabled to secure temporary monopolies by virtue of the high duties on tin plate and wire goods. The tariff co-operating with other influences has thus facilitated combination by limiting the area of competition.

The conditions, therefore, under which iron and steel have been produced in the United States have been favorable to a considerable degree of concentration. Fundamentally, it may be said that it was the co-operation of these conditions that developed the Steel Corporation. The geographical distribution of ores and coal favored the growth of the iron and steel industry in this country, and in large measure facilitated consolidation. The large capital necessary for the most economical production and the protective tariff, by shutting out foreign competition, tended to limit the domestic market to a relatively small number of great producers. The fluctuations of the trade, resulting in much waste and uncertainty, contributed still more to accentuate this growth toward concentration by increasing the desire among producers for some control over the industry.

The immediate cause of the formation of the Steel Corporation was a desire on the part of certain financial interests to secure some control over the iron and steel industry, and avert a threatened competition. By the close of the last century the bulk of the trade was already under the control of a few great consolidations or corporations. While some of these organizations had secured some measure of monopoly in their respective fields, the vicissitudes of the trade—especially the depression of the latter half of 1900—led to a threatened invasion on the part of some concerns of one another's fields. The organizations most vitally interested in this threatened invasion were the Carnegie Steel Company, the Federal Steel Company, the National Tube Company, and the American Steel and Wire Company. The outcome of this condition was a consolidation of these and other potential rivals into the United States Steel Corporation.

§ 3. By the formation of this great corporation more than half of the country's iron and steel production came under the control of a single organization. While the original purpose of the Steel Corporation was to avert threatened competition and exercise some measure of control over the steel industry of the United States, the conditions which fostered the tendency toward concentration have not operated, thus far, to promote permanent monopolization. The sources of raw material have not as yet come under the control of this organization. The Steel Corporation, like other great concerns engaged in the same business, owns or controls its sources of ore and coal supply. While holding some of the best ore lands in the Lake Superior region, it has not gained full possession of the productive forces of this district. Notwithstanding several additions to its holdings in this region, probably more than a fifth of the ore lands of the Lake Superior district are owned or held on lease by concerns in competition with it. The existence of considerable ore in other parts of the country under the control of independent companies renders any monopoly of the country's deposits of this material improbable in the immediate future.

Nor has the Steel Corporation, by virtue of its size, been enabled to secure control over the output of crude and finished products. The iron and steel industry requires large capital for the most economical production; but the principal economies seem to be achieved long before such a high capitalization as that of the Steel Corporation is reached. One of the officials of the Jones and Laughlin Steel Company declares that at least twenty or thirty million dollars are necessary to equip a steel plant for effective competition. The nominal capitalization of all the companies in the

United States, engaged in the manufacture of steel, is about two billion dollars, of which amount a billion and a half is represented by the Steel Corporation, and the remaining five hundred million by ten or twelve large companies. Notwithstanding the preponderating position of the Steel Corporation, its size apparently gives it no competitive advantage over its smaller rivals. During the six years of its history, it has absorbed other concerns, increased its holdings of ore and coal, and expended large sums on improvements and additions to plants. Yet its relative share of the country's output of iron and steel has shown no tendency to increase, and in some important lines of manufacture has even appreciably diminished. During its career its net earnings, while large, have not been extraordinary in comparison with its huge capitalization, and in view of the prosperity of the period during which it has existed. For more than two years these earnings were not deemed sufficient to pay dividends on the common stock.

The Steel Corporation, while organized to avert a threatened competition, has been compelled to withstand not a little rivalry. Outside of a few lines of manufacture guaranteed by patents it has achieved no monopoly. Paradoxical as it may seem, it is less of a monopoly than were some of the companies out of which it was formed. These companies, being consolidations of practically all the concerns of the country engaged in certain lines of production at the time of their formation, were enabled to control their markets. This control was safeguarded, so far as foreign competition was concerned, by the protective tariff. However, domestic competition soon developed; and by the time the Steel Corporation was organized much of this control was being undermined, and to-day most of it is entirely gone.

§ 4. In forming any estimate, therefore, of the stability of the corporation, its reaction on the conditions that gave it birth, and its probable future evolution, we must remember its character as a great, but not monopolistic organization. Its financial integrity and its influence on trade conditions do not rest upon any present control exercised over the steel industry. Its tendencies and significance for the future must be interpreted in the light of conditions which characterize the iron and steel trade as a whole.

Viewing the Steel Corporation as a competitive concern and at the same time the largest industrial organization in the world, the question of its financial stability is one of interest and significance. This organization started on its career with a capitalization in round numbers of $1,400,-000,000—several hundred millions more than the aggregate capitalization of all its constituent companies before they became parts of this great consolidation. Most of these companies were themselves capitalized on the basis of incomes earned during a period of prosperity, or of real or supposed monopoly achievement. This fact has tended to give the capitalization of the Steel Corporation a highly inflated aspect, and has seemed to make its ability to meet its corporate obligations extremely problematical. This capitalization, however, has been defended on the ground that the constituent companies, both before and after the organization of the Steel Corporation, have made several additions to their plants, and that their ore and coal properties have greatly increased in value. Indeed, the principal asset of the corporation is held to be its ore properties which, on account of the increasing use of steel, are becoming more and more valuable.

This defense has a certain basis of justification. The properties of the Steel Corporation are unquestionably more valuable to-day than they were at the time of its organization. Barring such contingencies as the discovery of new and extensive ore fields in other regions advantageously situated and cheaply worked, and the invention of new processes transforming the character of the steel industry, the holdings in the Lake Superior district will remain a most valuable asset. In capitalizing such a business, however, some discount should be made for the contingencies described. This is especially urgent in view of the fact that more than a third of the corporation's capital consists of a bonded debt whose obligations must be met during a period of depression as well as in normal and prosperous times. When it is remembered that the iron and steel industry is exposed to great vicissitudes in trade and that new discoveries and inventions may change its character and places of operation, it can hardly be said that the financial stability of the organization is fully assured. Viewed in the light of existing conditions, however, the assets of the Steel Corporation are unquestionably of great value. The critics of the financial policies of the corporation have probably more frequently underestimated its resources than the defenders have overestimated them.

§ 5. The Steel Corporation, while not a monopoly, has, nevertheless, reacted upon the conditions which favored its growth. Its career has been too short to justify any very sweeping generalizations in regard to this influence, but certain facts stand out in considerable prominence. Since the formation of this organization, the fluctuations in the prices of iron and steel have been less marked than in any other period of similar length since 1860. One of the most potent forces in the development of the tendency toward concentration of production has been these fluctuations incident to changes in demand. To reduce these oscillations in prices is an avowed purpose of the officials of the Steel Corporation. Controlling more than half the steel trade of the country, this organization has considerable influence on the policy of producers in fixing prices. In times of prosper-

ity it has pursued a conservative course in the matter of
raising prices; and independent concerns have found it to
their interest to follow suit. By keeping prices relatively
low in brisk times no inducements are offered to outsiders
to enter the industry as competitors. This policy renders
competition among those already in the field less severe in
times of depression. As a consequence prices have tended
toward greater uniformity.

The Steel Corporation is favored in the pursuit of this
policy by the fact that the steel industry of the country
is nearly all controlled by about a dozen concerns. All
these companies control most of their sources of raw material; and practically all the known deposits of ore are
held by them. By keeping the prices of finished material
in periods of prosperity at a low level, relative to those of
raw and crude products, producers who do not control their
own deposits of ore and aspire after more than a local market are virtually excluded. As a result of this policy there
would not be such a cutting of prices in a time of depression
as has heretofore proved so ruinous to many establishments
because more firms or companies had entered the industry
than the trade could support.

While the influence of the Steel Corporation has been in
the direction of greater stability of prices, its power to
achieve this end has been limited. It can exert an appreciable influence on trade in the way described, but it does
not control the productive forces of the industry. It is
still exposed in a considerable degree to the vicissitudes of
trade. While the officials of this organization disclaim any
intention of controlling the industry, it seems not improbable that they will seek to extend the corporation's influence. The holdings of the corporation in the Lake Superior region have been greatly increased since its formation; and efforts to augment them still further are likely to

be made.   This may indicate a desire ultimately to control
the trade by controlling the sources of raw material.   Such
a consummation, however, will be difficult of achievement.
Much of the Lake Superior district is held by independent
concerns which have no present intention of selling their
holdings.   These holdings and ore lands in other parts of
the country are sufficiently extensive to make it difficult for
any iron and steel consolidation to control the sources of
raw material.   Even were such control secured, the growing public sentiment against monopoly would probably
show itself in a clamor for abolition of tariff duties on iron
and steel.

§ 6. If the Steel Corporation secures fuller control over
the iron and steel industry of the United States in the near
future, it is likely to achieve this end in association with
other producers.   The industry is still exposed to great
changes in the demand for commodities; and the desire to
regulate production in accordance with these changes as
well as to secure monopolistic advantages will incite to
further attempts to gain control over the trade.   Such attempts have been made in various lines in the past by means
of pools or associations.   These organizations have had a
prominent place in the history of the industry; but in most
cases they have been weak on account of the number of
concerns involved, the consequent difficulty in securing harmony among the members, and the ease with which outside
capital could enter the field and break up the pool.   The
relatively small number of companies in the United States
now engaged in the steel trade on any large scale would
facilitate the making and keeping of agreements in regard
to production and prices.   The small number of concerns
engaged in the manufacture of steel rails accounts in large
measure for the success of the steel rail association, which
for six years has held the price of steel rails at $28.00 per

ton. In this association, as in others, the Steel Corporation with its large share of the country's trade has had a
preponderating influence. On account of the attitude of
public opinion and the more active enforcement of the anti-
trust laws many of these associations have been nominally
discontinued. Tacit understandings, however, in regard to
prices prevail now as ever, and seem nearly as effective as
definite pooling agreements.

What the influence of such associative action will be
upon the interests of consumers can only be conjectured.
The number of steel producers being relatively small, agreements or understandings in regard to prices will tend to be
more stable in the future than in the past. There may
be some marking up of prices as a result of such associative action; but the attempt to raise them much above
what market conditions would justify would in all likeli-
hood weaken the ties of the association, induce outside competitors to enter the field, and provoke much public opposition. In Germany the great coal syndicate has for these
reasons often resisted the movement to raise prices in
periods of prosperity. In this country at the present time
it is worthy of note that it is the Steel Corporation and not
the independent companies that is resisting the attempt to
raise prices. This opposition, of course, is due to the recognition of the importance of a steady rather than fluctuating volume of trade. Unless the steel industry becomes
monopolized by the Steel Corporation or some other combination having the sanction of the law, the interests of consumers do not seem to be menaced by the attempt to reduce the oscillations of the trade.

In the above outline it is seen that the Steel Corporation
is an expression of the centralizing tendencies of the iron
and steel industry, that it has assumed a certain position as

a result of these tendencies, and that it has reacted upon the conditions that gave it birth. In the following pages an examination of this organization will be made with the theory above outlined in view.

CHAPTER II

Determining Factors in the Iron and Steel Situation

§ 1. For an adequate appreciation of the forces which have evolved the United States Steel Corporation, and are fixing its character and economic position, some analysis is necessary of the determining factors in the iron and steel situation in this country. As has already been indicated several forces co-operated in the development of this great organization. However, the movement toward consolidation and the most salient features of this movement are the outcome principally of these four determining conditions: first, the natural distribution of ore and coal which made the growth of iron and steel manufacture in this country possible and favored in great measure large scale production; second, the nature of the industry which necessitated large capital for economical production; third, the fluctuating demand for goods which made some control over the trade peculiarly desirable from the standpoint of producers; fourth, the protective tariff which shut out effective foreign competition and acted as an inducement to the great producers to combine for the purpose of monopolistic control.

§ 2. A. For several years the United States has easily ranked first among the world's producers of iron and steel. This pre-eminence has in part been due to the productivity of the ore and coal fields with which the country is endowed. Through its ownership of land richly supplied with raw material, and by the application of large capital to

25

both mining and manufacture, this country has been enabled to supply nearly all the home markets and to export large quantities of iron and steel goods.

Of the world's production of iron ore in 1903—estimated by the American Iron and Steel Association to have been about 100,198,000 tons [1]—the United States produced 35,019,308 tons, or about 34.95 per cent. The countries next in rank were Germany and Great Britain, which contributed respectively, 21.19 per cent and 13.96 per cent. In the same year this country produced 18,009,252 tons of pig iron, or 38.83 per cent of the world's total, and 14,534,978 tons of steel, or 40.57 per cent. The production for 1904 fell off somewhat on account of the depression of that year, the output of pig iron in this country having declined to 16,497,033 tons, and that of steel, to 13,767,306 tons. The years 1905 and 1906 were years of unsurpassed prosperity in the iron and steel trade, not only in this country but in Europe as well. It is estimated that the output of pig iron in the United States during 1906 reached 25,850,000 tons; in Germany, 12,300,000 (metric) tons; and in Great Britain, 10,100,000 tons.[2] The tonnage of steel in this country for 1905 attained the enormous total of 19,912,757.[3]

From these figures it will be seen that the United States in recent years has been producing a large proportion of the world's iron and steel. Whether or not this country will continue to retain this preëminence for a long period is doubtful. Much depends upon the country's deposits of workable ore; and these have been variously estimated from a little over 1,000,000,000 to more than 4,000,000,000 tons. The first of these estimates is probably much too low.

[1] *Iron Age*, Sept. 14, 1905. Unless otherwise indicated in this work, the word tons means gross tons.

[2] *Ibid.*, Dec. 20, 1906, p. 1683.

[3] *Ibid.*, March 22, 1906, p. 1042.

While an estimate of this character is necessarily very un-certain, it may serve as a rough indication of the probable limits of our ore capacity. The ore fields of Germany, in-cluding Luxemburg, are thought to contain over 2,000,000,-000 tons. Recent discoveries credit China with ore de-posits of great magnitude. These large and less developed fields are likely in the near future to be worked at a much lower cost than those in this country, as they are to a great extent surface deposits and as labor cost is less than here. With the gradual exhaustion of the more superficial de-posits, the law of diminishing returns will make itself felt sooner or later in the United States; and prices here will tend to be higher than in regions which have been more recently worked. The position of the United States as the leading producer of iron and steel will, however, probably be preserved for many years.

B. The iron and steel industry in this country has de-veloped mainly in the states east of the Mississippi River. Within this region are the principal coal and iron-ore dis-tricts of the country and the chief markets for iron and steel goods. Outside of this region the known fields of ore and coal are either too limited or too unfavorably situated for the assembling of material seriously to affect the present trade of the country. Within the section mentioned, iron and steel manufacture is carried on principally in two dis-tricts: a region extending from New York and New Jersey on the east to Illinois on the west, and the country about Birmingham, Alabama. The first of these is much the larger in extent and productivity, and contains most of the plants of the Steel Corporation. The existence of large manufacturing establishments in this region is due to the proximity of extensive coking-coal fields, to the nearness of excellent markets, and to cheap transportation facilities over the great lakes from the ore regions of Minnesota and Michigan.

Pennsylvania, which is the center of the industry in the United States, easily leads in the amount and value of her products. In 1900—the year before the formation of the Steel Corporation—the value of the iron and steel manufactured in this State constituted fifty-four per cent of that of the entire country. In 1905 Pennsylvania produced forty-six per cent of all the pig iron and fifty-five per cent of all the steel made in the United States.[1] This predominance is to be attributed to the natural advantages of the state in the matter of coal deposits and limestone, to the easy communication with the Lake Superior ore fields, and to its excellent position as a distributing center for the eastern part of the country. Toward the east and south of Pittsburg is the famous Connellsville coking-coal region. The importance of this district to the iron industry of Pennsylvania is seen in the fact that in 1905 63.8 per cent of all the coke produced in this country came from this state.

Ohio ranks next to Pennsylvania in the amount and value of her iron and steel products. Illinois, New Jersey, Indiana, West Virginia, and New York are also producers in this northern section. The industry in Ohio and West Virginia may be regarded as western and southern extensions of that of western Pennsylvania. The trade in West Virginia is due also in part to the noted Pocahontas coal district. The industry in Illinois and Indiana has developed largely on account of the excellent market for iron and steel goods in Chicago and the West. These states are also in close proximity to the ore supplies of the Lake Superior region. The mills of New Jersey and New York are largely mills for the manufacture of finished material and are located for easy distribution to eastern markets.

The iron and steel manufacture of Alabama is entirely

[1] *Bulletin* of the American Iron and Steel Association, Dec., 1906.

separate from the industry of the northern section. Its development has been due to purely natural causes,—closely adjacent supplies of iron ore and coal. The facility with which these essentials to iron manufacture can be assembled and the cheapness of labor bring the cost of production down to a lower level here than in any other part of the Union. Mills and furnaces in some instances get both their ore and coal within half a mile of the plant. While Alabama is thus favored with productive facilities, her development has not been so rapid as that of the Lake states—a fact which may be partly attributed to her remoteness from the best markets of the country. Present indications, however, point to a great future development of the industry in this region.

The iron and steel industry of the country is carried on mainly in these two regions. The first, which is much the more extensive and important, draws its supplies of raw material from the ore fields of the Lake Superior district and the coal fields of Pennsylvania and West Virginia, and depends upon the cheap transportation of the Great Lakes for the assembling of material. To a considerable extent the producers of this region sell in the same markets. Geographical proximity thus brings them into certain relationships with each other; and both community of interests and competition have favored combination. The second is centered mainly in Alabama, and depends upon the ore and coal of that State. Its markets are limited for the most part to the South; and it has therefore had much less commercial influence and a more restricted growth than the northern section.

C. The most important natural condition affecting the status of the iron and steel industry is the supply of ore. Iron ore is found in appreciable quantities in half the states of the Union. Considerable deposits are known to exist in some of the Rocky Mountain and Pacific Coast states, notably in Colorado and Utah.[1]   Many of these ore lands are owned by the Colorado Fuel & Iron Company. Extensive areas of ore deposits are found in the Atlantic States, especially in Pennsylvania, which up to the early eighties was the chief ore producing state in the country. The main supply of the country, however, is derived from the Lake Superior region, which during the last six years has produced over seventy per cent of the country's total. Owing to the fact that this ore contains a larger percentage of iron than the ores of the South and West, the proportion of iron derived from the Lake Superior district would, during these years, exceed four-fifths.   During the last two years the proportion of ore supplied by this region has increased.   Of the 42,526,133 tons of ore mined in the United States in 1905, 34,522,965 tons were shipped from this district; and the proportion for 1906 is even greater.

This ore region is located along the southern and western shores of Lake Superior, principally in Minnesota and Michigan.   Most of the mines are within a hundred miles of the Lake coast, from which easy and cheap transport is made to the lower lake ports.   The extent of the deposits of this region has been variously estimated; but most recent estimates place it at upwards of 2,000,000,000 tons.[2]

The next most important ore district of the United States is the Alabama region upon which the iron interests of that section depend.   At the time the Twelfth Census was taken Alabama ranked third among the states in the production of iron ore and fifth in the production of coal.   Its rank

[1] For account of ore deposits in Utah, see *Iron Age*, Oct. 27, 1904, p. 3.

[2] Richard H. Edmonds, in *Review of Reviews*, Dec., 1906.   For an interesting account of consolidation in this region, see H. R. Mussey, *Combination in the Mining Industry*, in the *Columbia Studies in History, Economics and Public Law*.

as a producer of ore remains the same to-day. Notwithstanding this high rank the output of the state is rather
small compared with · that of Minnesota or Michigan.
Nevertheless the possibilities of the Alabama region are
great. While the extent of its ore fields is much less than
those of the Lake Superior district, the facilities for assembling material make the cost of utilizing the ore less
than at the North. Owing to differences in the character
of their products, the iron interests of Alabama have not,
thus far, come into serious competition with the industries
depending for their supply of ore upon the Lake Superior
region. It seems not unlikely, however, that these interests
with their facilities for cheap production will at no distant
day be rivals of the great combinations of the North.

The Lake Superior and Alabama regions are estimated to
contain at least ninety per cent of the workable ore of the
country. While such an estimate is necessarily uncertain,
it seems probable that these two regions will supply the
bulk of our native ore for many years to come.

The ores of these two districts differ in certain noteworthy particulars. While high and low grade ores are
found in both regions, the percentage of iron contained in
the Lake Superior material which it has been profitable to
mine ranges from fifty-two to sixty-seven, while that of
the Alabama product averages about forty-five. The Lake
Superior product which is ordinarily utilized is thus richer
in the proportion of iron contents.

Another difference of more vital importance is the variation in the percentage of phosphorus contained in the ore.
On this difference depends the suitability of the material
for the manufacture of Bessemer steel. Ores containing
more than five or six hundredths of one per cent of phosphorus are unavailable for the Bessemer process. The Lake
Superior product varies on the average from one hundredth

to fifteen hundredths of one per cent, while the Alabama ores contain from one-tenth of one per cent to one per cent. Much of the former, therefore, is suitable for the manufacture of Bessemer steel, while the latter is not. The open-hearth process, however, is being used to manufacture steel from more phosphoric ores; and the development of this process seems to be neutralizing the importance of this difference in the ores of the two regions. The steadily increasing demand for open-hearth steel is also noticeable. The following table shows the increased production of steel both of the Bessemer and open-hearth grades for the years 1900-1905:[1]

	Open-hearth steel. Gross tons.	Bessemer steel. Gross tons.	Total for country. Gross tons.	Per cent of open hearth.
1900	3,398,135	6,684,770	10,082,905	34
1901	4,656,309	8,713,302	13,369,611	35
1902	5,687,729	9,138,363	14,826,092	38
1903	5,829,911	8,592,829	14,422,740	40
1904	5,908,166	7,859,140	13,767,306	43
1905	8,971,376	10,941,375	19,912,751	45

The steady increase of the production of open-hearth steel is noticeable, and its increasing relative importance is significant. The fact that this product seems fully the equal of the Bessemer material,[2] and is even supplanting it, has allayed much of the fear once felt concerning the effects of the possible monopolization of the Lake Superior region.

From this brief consideration of the ore and coal districts of the country and of the industries depending upon these districts, it will be seen that natural conditions have determined the location of iron and steel plants. The great combinations of these regions have been formed among corporations either engaged in different stages of the manu-

---

[1] *Iron Age*, Mar. 22, 1906, p. 1042.

[2] *Ibid.*, Feb. 8, 1906, p. 513. See account of meeting of American Society of Civil Engineers.

facture of the same class or classes of commodities in one or other of these regions, or depending upon the same sources of raw material and competing in the same markets. In neither district has the trade been monopolized. In the North, where consolidations have attained their greatest development, there is still much competition. The ore and coal fields have thus far proved too extensive for monopolization. Even if these fields should come under a single control, there would still be much effective competition from the South, and possibly from the West.

§ 3. *A.* Another factor of prime importance in determining the iron and steel situation is the large capital necessary for economical production. This condition has favored the formation of large corporations. The fact that only large concerns can compete successfully tends to limit the number of producers and facilitates combination among these producers. In order to form some estimate of the influence of this condition we may note, first, the fact of concentration, and then consider the question of the economies achieved.

The tendency toward concentration has been very marked during the last two or three decades. During this period an increasing amount of capital has been used to equip properly blast furnaces and rolling mills, and secure requisite mining and transportation facilities. The acquisition of mining and transportation facilities was not considered essential to an efficiently organized manufacturing company until the later nineties; but it is now almost indispensable to a corporation aspiring after more than local trade. The trend toward more elaborate equipment can be seen in a comparison between the number of iron and steel establishments and the amount of capital invested. During the twenty years from 1880 to 1900 the number of active blast furnaces in the United States declined from 341 to 224. The amount of capital invested in blast furnaces—including rented property—increased in the same period from $89,531,362 to $148,226,113.[1] In other words considerably more than twice as much money was expended in the equipment of the average blast furnace in 1900 than in 1880. The number of active establishments producing steel ingots or castings and rolled iron and steel numbered in 1880, 358; and in 1900, 438. The capital invested increased from $116,458,390 to $441,795,983.[2] Thus, while the number of rolling mills and steel works increased during these two decades less than twenty per cent, the capital invested was augmented by nearly three hundred per cent.

This trend in the direction of concentration in the steel trade may be illustrated by organizations in rail manufacture. In 1887 the first rail pool was organized; and this combination consisted of fifteen members. At first it was weak, owing to considerable outside competition, and also to internal dissatisfaction with the allotments of trade. In the allotment of 1888, the largest percentage granted to any one company was 13.5; and this share was given to the Carnegie Company. In 1897, ten years after the formation of the first pool, this rail association consisted of but six members. The only considerable manufacturer of steel rails outside of the pool was the Illinois Steel Company, which did not enter this association on account of the Illinois laws against pooling. In the allotment of 1897 the Carnegie Company was given 53.50 per cent of the pool's trade, and the Lackawanna Company, nearly two-fifths of the remainder. Thus within a single decade the number of companies producing steel rails on any considerable scale was reduced, and the tendency of the industry to come under the control of a few large corporations became more

[1] *Twelfth Census*, vol. 10, p. 29.   [2] *Ibid.*, vol. 10, p. 54.

and more apparent. Since the spring of 1901, nearly three-fifths of the steel rails manufactured in the United States have been produced by the constituent companies of the Steel Corporation; and the remainder, principally by five companies,—the Lackawanna, the Bethlehem, the Cambria, the Pennsylvania, and the Maryland, of which the most important is the Lackawanna.

Another indication of this drift toward large corporate ownership is seen in the number of abandoned establishments. In 1900, according to the Twelfth Census, there were 123 iron and steel establishments with a total capital of $23,831,819 reported idle. This was the largest idle investment shown for any industry. Such an abandonment of industrial establishments is significant both of the shifting location of the iron industry and of the increasing concentration in large plants. In many states there exist abandoned mills which were built to utilize a local supply of ore and which have been rendered permanently unproductive by the competition of new mills, either better equipped, or in proximity to superior raw materials.

The tendency toward large-scale production has not only been in the direction of larger and better equipped blast furnaces and mills, but also in the direction of consolidation of plants and companies. This trend is exemplified in two kinds of combinations: the union of concerns engaged in different stages of the production of a class or classes of commodities; and the consolidation of companies manufacturing the same grades or classes of articles. An example of the former would be the Federal Steel Company, organized in 1898, and now a part of the Steel Corporation. This company consisted principally of the Minnesota Iron Company owning ore fields in the Lake Superior region and manufacturing crude iron, the Elgin, Joliet and Eastern

Railroad Company providing certain transportation facilities to some of the coal regions of Illinois, and the Illinois Steel Company manufacturing crude material like bars, slabs, etc., and some finished products like steel rails. Such a union is formed to secure a higher degree of productive efficiency by adjusting more economically the production of raw and crude material to the demand for finished goods. An example of a consolidation manufacturing the same grade of articles would be the American Tinplate Company, also merged in the Steel Corporation. This company consisted of more than forty rival concerns. A combination of this character generally aims to restrict or destroy competition, although economy of production may also be sought. An indication of the extent to which this integration of industries in both these directions has gone is seen in the fact that nearly all the great steel concerns of the country are producers of raw, crude, and finished material, and that more than half the country's trade is now controlled by a single corporation.

B. The progress of this concentration has been due in part to the fact that increasing returns have resulted from the application of large capital. To-day it is practically impossible to carry on an extensive manufacturing business in the higher and more important grades of iron and steel goods with a capital of less than fifteen million dollars. This fact may be illustrated by considering the cost of such an item as a modern blast furnace. Such a furnace is likely to be from 500 to 700 tons capacity. A rough estimate is, to the effect that a 500 ton furnace costs about $500,000, and takes upward of a year and a half to build.[1] In addition to this investment, the labor of some hundreds of men and the transportation of 1,500 tons or more of

---

[1] *Report of Industrial Commission*, vol. 1, p. 945.

material must be provided for each day. This of itself requires a capital of half a million. In other words it would take about $1,000,000 capital to build, start, and keep in operation a single 500 ton furnace. The cost of producing a ton of pig iron in such a furnace is from forty to fifty per cent less than in the average furnace of the early eighties, which represented an investment of $250,000 to $300,000.

Plants with large capital have thus supplanted those with small capital because of their superior efficiency and economy. How far production on an enlarging scale continues to be more economical it is difficult to determine. The application of repeated " doses " of capital does not necessarily continue indefinitely to be more economical. The point on this enlarging scale at which the most efficient production is reached varies with conditions. Under similar conditions, a capital of forty or fifty millions would, in the opinion of one of the officials of the Steel Corporation whom the writer interviewed, be as efficient in the iron and steel industry as a capital of ten times that amount. One of the witnesses before the Industrial Commission testified that a capital of $20,000,000 to $30,000,000 would build and equip a steel plant for effective competition.[1] It would seem from these statements that the principal economies achieved in the industry by large investment of capital can be attained with less than $50,000,000. With capital of this amount or more a steel concern can own and equip the most efficient blast furnaces and mills and secure control of its sources of raw material.

C. The question whether or not a corporation whose capital is many times this amount has any competitive advantage merely by virtue of its size is difficult to answer. To this

[1] *Report of Industrial Commission*, vol. 13, pp. 504-106.

question certain steel officials, as has already been noted, have given a negative reply. There are, however, some considerations which seem to favor a large consolidation. The well known savings in the matter of advertising and in the employment of a smaller number of traveling agents and salesmen are worthy of mention, although these economies are not so marked as in the case of some other industries. The amount of capital employed for advertising and agency purposes in the iron and steel trade is small compared with the total investment. A more important item of economy is found in the organization of the mills consolidated. In concentrating departments of manufacture, for example, instead of compelling each establishment to make numerous sizes and parts of the same product considerable saving can be made. Stopping a mill to change the rolls to suit each size or variety of a commodity involves waste of time. This waste is obviated when the different sizes and shapes are distributed among a number of mills whose productive work need not be interrupted. In many of the more finished varieties of iron and steel goods the estimated saving through this multiplicity of mills amounts to more than one dollar per ton.

It may be said in general that the iron and steel trade from its very nature demands large capital. To some extent productive efficiency seems to be increased by consolidation. Increasing returns have in large measure followed increasing outlays. It is improbable, however, that this law of increasing returns operates indefinitely. As has already been noted the principal economies attained by an iron and steel concern are achieved with a capital of less than $50,000,000. There are some savings, as has also been indicated, in the multiplicity of mills in cases where the capital may exceed this limit. It is unlikely, however, that any considerable economies are gained by very large con-

solidations by virtue of mere size. The fact that the Steel
Corporation, as will be noted later, has not increased its
proportion of the country's trade during the six years of
its existence is some evidence of the truth of this assumption.
The necessity of large capital to equip properly a steel concern limits the number of such organizations. This facilitates
combination for the purpose of controlling the industry.
The motive for organizing the larger consolidations is not,
therefore, competitive efficiency but the desire for monopoly
control.

§ 4. *A*. The third great factor in the iron and steel situation furnishes a powerful incentive toward combination for
the purpose of control. This factor is the varying demand
for commodities. Alternating periods of prosperity and
depression act with great force upon this industry, and
make some control over the trade peculiarly desirable
from the standpoint of producers. The demand for iron
and steel varies, not according to the pressing needs of consumers, but according to changes in the development of new
enterprises. These changes are periodic; and this period-
icity is closely associated with variations in the spirit of
investment. In so-called good times new enterprises of all
sorts are freely launched. In succeeding periods of dull-
ness comparatively few ventures are entered upon. But
investment and fresh ventures imply the erection of plants
and the increased use of tools and machines. These in
turn mean iron and steel.

The heaviest consumers, too, of iron and steel, like railroad corporations, purchase their material in large shipment, and this material is intended to supply a need for
many years ahead. The demand is generally great with
the advent of prosperous times or when confidence is
felt in the future. It is then that liberal outlays can be
made for the improvement of stock and for embarking upon

new enterprises. If steel cars are to be substituted for wooden ones, they are ordered by the scores and hundreds; if a new railroad is to be built, shipments of rails must be made in thousands of tons. During periods of depression, on the other hand, little iron and steel is ordered beyond the maintenance of plants and stocks. Old material, if servicable at all, is likely to continue in use until the outlook points to the return of more prosperous times.

Until very recently these fluctuations have been accentuated by the influence of intermediate producers. The demand for finished products varies considerably and with great uncertainty from year to year. From the mining of ore to the sale of finished products there are several stages of manufacture and transportation. The intermediate producers must adjust their scale of production—which, for obvious reasons, cannot be immediately enlarged or contracted—to a changeable and often fitful demand on the part of consumers of finished products. This adjustment is necessarily very imperfectly made where the intermediate producers are independent concerns. This fact has made the combination under one control of all the stages of production from the mining of raw material to the sale of finished goods desirable and economical. This integrated system is becoming characteristic of nearly all the larger consolidations of the iron and steel trade.

B. These oscillations of the industry are reflected in variations of prices. In December, 1898, steel rails were selling as low as $17.00 per ton. A year later the price had risen to $35.00 per ton. In another year the price had declined to $26.00 per ton. Steel billets on December 29, 1898, were quoted at $16.25 per ton; on November 29, 1899, at $39.50 per ton; and on October 3, 1900, at $16.50 per ton. The lowest and highest quotations for wire rods during the years 1898 to 1900 inclusive, were respectively

$20.00 and $50.00 per ton. After the latter price had been reached early in 1900, there was a drop to $30.00 per ton before the close of the year.

Unstable prices necessarily cause great variations in earnings. The income of the Republic Iron and Steel Company during the two prosperous years of 1900 and 1901 is fairly typical of what one is likely to find in a trade marked by great and uncertain changes in the demand for goods. This company showed on its books for the year ending June 30, 1901, a total of $51,000,000 assets. Its capital stock was $47,497,000, of which $20,306,000 was preferred. In 1900 the company's net earnings were $5,684,101, and in 1901, only $1,034,248. The amounts paid out in dividends for the two years were $3,643,729 and $309,099 respectively.[1] This falling off means that in 1901, which was generally regarded as a good year, the Republic Iron and Steel Company paid out in dividends only one-twelfth of what it had paid in 1900, and only a little over one-fifth of the amount needed to cover the seven per cent dividends on its preferred stock, leaving nothing at all for the common stock.

The vicissitudes in the demand for railroad supplies are strikingly shown in the experience of the Pressed Steel Car Company. This organization from 1899 to 1903 more than earned large dividends on its full stock—its common stock securing twenty-eight per cent in 1902. In 1904, however, it had so little business, less than one-seventh that of 1902, that it was obliged to draw heavily on its surplus to pay the dividends on its preferred stock and was compelled to pass the dividends on the common.[2]

[1] *Report of the British Iron Trade Commission on American Industrial Conditions*, p. 300.

[2] *Iron Age*, Feb. 23, 1905, p. 655.

The experience of the Pressed Steel Car Company is illustrative of the fact that the more specialized a phase of the iron and steel industry is the more exposed it is to the vicissitudes of the trade. The larger consolidations, in addition to securing control of their sources of raw material and the stages of manufacture from raw to finished product, have embraced under their control several different lines of manufacture. By thus extending their markets these combinations have to some extent steadied their profits. The greater the number of markets the more certain the income is likely to be.

C. This desire to lessen the fluctuations of the industry has been a leading incentive to consolidation. The necessity of opening up and shutting down mills and furnaces with varying periods of demand causes much waste. The mechanical waste involved is great enough to increase appreciably the cost of production. But this is not the only loss. Brisk times are periods of high money wages. The attempt to curtail expenses in times of severe depression by lowering wages meets with resistance from workmen—especially labor unions. The demand for increased remuneration during flourishing periods and resistance to any curtailment in dull times with consequent strikes and lockouts have been sources of great loss to iron and steel establishments. Another feature of the situation giving rise to waste is what may be called a tendency to abnormal competition. During a period of prosperity—especially if long continued—an unduly large number of competitors are induced to enter the field. With the advent of dull times there is great " slashing " of prices among these rival concerns to secure trade. This competition frequently causes prices to sink below the level of cost, and many establishments are driven out of business with consequent loss of capital. This feature of the industry has not only caused

waste, but has tended to accentuate the naturally great oscillations of the trade.

The uncertainties and fluctuations of the business have
been responsible for another characteristic of the industry.
The prices at which the securities of steel concerns have
been sold have been relatively low and very fluctuating.
Men put money into the iron and steel business, not as an
investment, but as a means of making a fortune. Steel
stock was thus a favorite with speculators rather than investors; and the industry as a whole was permeated with a
speculative spirit.

One of the great ends of consolidation has been to reduce
the waste incident to fluctuation and to render returns
steadier and more certain. Such an aim could not be
achieved without an organization controlling a large percentage of the trade of the country. If the organization of
the Steel Corporation is to be attributed to any one cause
more than another, it is to be assigned to the desire of
achieving this end and placing the industry on an investment level.

§ 5. *A.* Another determining influence acting on the iron
and steel trade of the country and an important factor in
facilitating combination has been the protective tariff. It
is not the purpose of this dissertation to enter into any
detailed discussion of such an intricate subject as the
relation of the tariff to the growth of the iron and steel
manufacture, but simply to indicate the nature of that relation, especially in its bearing upon the growth of consolidation.

It has frequently been asserted that one of the chief causes
of combination is the protective tariff. Mr. Havemeyer's
dictum that the tariff is the mother of the trusts has many
supporters. It may be doubted, however, if this assertion
is to be taken without reserve. In this country some of

the largest and most monopolistic combinations have no direct tariff protection; and in England, where there is no protection, combinations have been formed and operated with success. At the same time many consolidations in this country would never have been organized without the tariff. The restriction which the tariff places upon foreign competition has acted as an incentive to combination where industrial conditions were in other respects favorable. Whether or not such a combination secures permanent control over the domestic market depends upon circumstances. If a consolidation secures control of the sources of raw material within the protected area, and a tariff is levied upon such material imported from foreign countries, it is clear that domestic competition has lost in part at least its power to lower prices. Without such control or some other monopolistic advantage within the country itself, the tariff will not give a business organization a permanent monopoly. A combination of all the manufacturers of a nation may secure a temporary control of the market; but new capital will enter the field and reduce prices to a competitive level.

It is true that trust officials in those industries where high tariffs are levied are generally strong defenders of protection. Among several reasons usually cited by them for the maintenance of a high tariff is one directly opposed to the assertion that monopoly is thereby fostered. It is contended that protection should be maintained, as its withdrawal would involve the ruin of competing organizations and thus leave the domestic field in the possession of combinations. The validity of this contention, which has gained a certain popularity, is difficult to see. If a consolidation achieves economies by which it can sell goods more cheaply than its smaller competitors, it can hardly be said that the alleged more expensive methods of

those competitors should be encouraged by a tariff. The
public is concerned with securing cheap products of good
quality whether produced by a large or a small concern.
If a large organization, by virtue of its size, can manufacture at a cost sufficiently low to meet foreign competition, but its smaller rivals need tariff protection, it is evident that the public derives no benefit from the economies
achieved by the combination in safeguarding its rivals by
protective measures.

Upon the iron and steel industry of the United States
the tariff has exercised considerable influence. Until very
recently the cost of manufacturing iron and steel has been,
in general, higher in this country than in Europe; and an
important part of this expense has been labor cost. The
contention of manufacturers that the abolition of the
tariff would necessitate the payment of lower wages in the
industry has not been without some basis of fact. The
tariff has protected the American industry by neutralizing
the advantages which foreign producers had in the matter
of lower costs.

It may be said further that protective duties on raw and
crude material have restricted the area of competition within the United States. Hermann Levy has shown that im-
port duties on pig-iron have worked injury to steel establishments east of the Alleghanies, which at one time were
dependent on foreign producers for their raw and crude
material.[1] The tariff of forty cents per ton on iron ore is
probably sufficient to prevent the establishment of iron and
steel plants on the Atlantic sea-board, which could easily secure cheap raw material from Nova Scotia, Spain, and
Cuba. This duty, moreover, would be an important safe-

[1] Levy, *Die Stahlindustrie der Vereinigten Staaten von Amerika*, II.

guard to any concern which secured control of all the best ore fields of the country.

While the tariff has thus restricted the area of competition, no consolidation has, as yet, secured a permanent monopoly in any of the more important branches of the iron and steel trade. The ore and coal fields of the country have thus far proved too extensive for monopolization; and no control has been secured over transportation. Internal competition has thus been free to act and has often been sufficient to reduce prices to a point very near the European level. The tariff has acted as a stimulus to combination, and has enabled organizations to secure temporary monopolies. In such cases new capital has entered the field, and has soon destroyed the control that had been achieved over market conditions.

B. A fair illustration of the working of the tariff in the iron and steel trade is the career of the tin plate industry from 1890 to the time of the organization of the United States Steel Corporation. This industry in this country is generally cited as a product of protection. The development of tin plate manufacture in the United States may be said to date from the enactment of the McKinley Bill. Previous to 1890 practically all the tin plate used in this country was imported. An industry of hardly any significance underwent great development almost immediately after the enactment of the McKinley law.

The method of manufacturing tin plate is rather simple, so far as process is concerned; but considerable skill is required to turn out good plates. By tin plate is meant a thin sheet of steel or iron coated with tin. The standard size of these plates is 14 x 20 inches. These plates are usually placed in boxes containing 225 sheets and weighing 108 pounds each. What is called terne plate—an allied product—is a similar sheet of steel or iron covered with an alloy of lead and tin, generally two-thirds lead and one-third tin.

Before the enactment of the McKinley Bill, the tin plate industry in the United States had been maintaining a struggling existence. Though protected by a duty of one cent per pound on the foreign product, American tin plate was not in a position to withstand English competition. The competitive strength of the industry depended mainly upon three things: the price of pig tin, the price of steel, and the labor cost. In regard to the price of pig tin, the English manufacturer did not seem to have any special advantage over the American producer. Block tin was sold about as cheaply in New York as in London.[1] The reason for the high price in London, notwithstanding its proximity to Cornwall, is that the Cornish mines did not supply the entire English demand, and the price was governed by the quotations of tin from Australia and the Strait Settlements. Regarding the price of steel the advantage in 1890 was with the English manufacturer. By the middle nineties, however, Bessemer steel bars, which were used in both countries, sold about twenty per cent cheaper in the United States than in England. The prices per ton in these two countries in April, 1896, were $15.50 and $18.70 respectively. In the matter of labor cost the American manufacturer was handicapped in the early history of the industry by the high price of labor and the lack of technical knowledge. These difficulties were partially overcome by the middle nineties, as considerable technical skill had been developed, and wages, owing to the depression of 1893, had fallen some fifteen per cent. Nevertheless, the disparity in

[1] On Mar. 4, 1898, the quotations in London and New York were $311.10 and $310.44 per ton respectively. Variations before and after this time seem to have been about the same.

labor cost was great. According to Sir R. Giffen, the Welsh laborer in the tin plate industry received on the average, in 1897, $5.46 (£1 2s 5d) per week, while the Pennsylvania workman, whose efficiency was no greater, received $10.68 per week. The advantage, therefore, in respect to labor cost was greatly in favor of the English producer.

Taken all in all, the English manufacturer could make tin plate nearly thirty per cent cheaper than the American, and this at a time when the expense of production in this country was at a very low point. For the English producer, the price per box at the factory reached as low as $2.20; and a box could be delivered in New York, freight paid, for about $2.50. The cost of American tin plate of first class material was not below $2.75 per box. Without a tariff duty, therefore, the English product could easily undersell the American material; but in the middle nineties when wages in the United States were very low, a low duty was sufficient to enable the native producer to compete with the foreign merchant.

In 1890, owing to the high price of steel bars and the high wages of labor combined with a very imperfect knowledge of technical processes American tin plate sold in New York City for $5.50 per box while the English product sold for $3.88 plus $1.08 of tariff duty. The price of English tin plate was considerably above cost, but the American manufacturer being unable to offer any competition, a price of nearly $5.00 per box was paid by the American consumer for the imported product.

With the enactment of the McKinley Bill, the duty on foreign tin and terne plate was increased to 2.2 cents per pound, or about $2.37 per box. For the first time in our history, American tin plate was enabled to undersell the English product in the home market. The clause relating to tin and terne plate in the McKinley law went into effect

July 1, 1891. From that date the imported material was gradually supplanted by the native product. The imports of tin and terne plates in 1890 were 737,955,079 pounds; in 1891, 734,425,267 pounds. By 1897 the importations had declined to 230,073,683 pounds.[1] Contemporaneous with this decline, was an increasing production of tin plate in the United States. In 1890, the amount produced was negligible. In 1892, it reached 13,646,719 pounds. In the following year, the native product increased to 99,819,-212 pounds; and by 1897 the amount of tin and terne plate produced in the United States was 446,982,063 pounds.

The tin plate industry in the United States may be said, therefore, to date from the time when the McKinley tariff act went into effect, and seems to have been intimately related to it. It is to be remembered, however, that this tariff bill was one of three or four contributing causes of the growth of the industry. As has already been noted, the price of steel and labor cost declined greatly during the first half of the nineties. This decline enabled the American manufacturer to hold the home market when the Wilson Act of 1894 reduced the duty on tin plate to 1.2 cents per pound, or about $1.30 per box. In 1897 the Dingley Act raised the duty to 1.5 cents per pound, thus rendering the American manufacturer somewhat more secure. The tariffs, therefore, since 1890 have been sufficient to give protection to the industry in the United States, and may be said to have stimulated its growth. At the time when the price of steel and the cost of labor were very low in this country, the English manufacturer was still able, without the tariff, to undersell his American competitor. It was the tariff, co-operating with the declining price of

[1] For effect on the Welsh tin-plate mills, see *Consular Reports* for May, 1896, pp. 67 and 68; November, 1897, p. 323; and May, 1898.

steel and low labor cost, which enabled the tin plate industry to take root on American soil.

During the early and middle nineties the price of American tin plate steadily declined. Under the protection of the tariff the number of plants increased to over forty; and competition among these, co-operating with improvements in processes, low wages, and cheap steel, brought the price of the American product down to $2.70 per box, at mill, in 1898.[1] Toward the end of this year and the beginning of 1899, the cost of production was being raised on account of the increased prices of steel and pig tin. About the same time, the encouraging prospects of the industry incident to the revival of trade toward the close of the decade, seemed threatened by the competition of an increasing number of plants engaged in the business. Early in 1898 negotiations were opened to ascertain if it were possible to form a company that could control all the plants of the country. As a result of these negotiations, the American Tin Plate Company was formed in December, 1898, embracing nearly all the plants of the country.

This industry was now virtually in the hands of a monopoly. The new company endeavored to secure itself from outside competition by agreements with merchants and producers of raw material and by patents on the latest devices in machinery. In this attempt the company was for a time measurably successful. The Dingley tariff imposing a duty of 1.5 cents per pound on imported tin and terne plate protected this monopoly from foreign competition.

In January, 1899, the price of tin plate was increased from $2.70 per hundred pound box at the mill to $3.00; and before summer it had been raised to $3.50. Imported tin plate could not be sold in this country for less than $4.00

---

[1] *Tin and Terne.* Jan. 26, 1898.

per hundred pound box, although English plate was selling at Liverpool at $2.30 per box. The rise in the price of the American product cannot be attributed to any increase in labor cost, as wages and salaries remained low and in some cases were reduced.[1] The price of tin had increased, but not more so than for the English producer. While the price of steel was rising during the early months of 1899, this rise did not greatly increase the relative cost of production for the American manufacturer. The English manufacturer was affected by the rise, though to a less extent. The principal element, moreover, in the expense of production was labor cost; and this had not yet increased. The increased price of American tin plate, therefore, must be attributed to a combination which had achieved a temporary monopoly, the power of which was in a measure safe-guarded by a protective tariff.

The tariff was thus a contributing factor in the development of the American tin plate industry and an important aid to consolidation. It has not been, however, a complete protector of monopoly where the possibilities of home competition have not been greatly reduced. This was shown in the later history of the American Tin Plate Company. Notwithstanding the measures taken to control the domestic trade, by the time the Steel Corporation had formed in 1901, several independent tin plate mills were being built; and at present these independent concerns are increasing their trade at the expense of the older organization,[2] which has been merged with the American Sheet Steel Company.

What has been said concerning the influence of the tariff on the tin plate industry and combination can be said with

[1] *Tin and Terne*, Jan. 12, 1899.
[2] *Iron Age*, Jan. 3, 1907, p. 65.

certain modifications concerning other branches of the iron and steel trade. The tariff by shutting out foreign competition enabled the home industry to grow, and by limiting the field of competition facilitated the formation of combinations whose object, if not achievement, has been monopoly. The careers of these combinations, however, have been illustrations of the persistence of competition. No sooner were these organizations formed than new capital entered the industry in competition with them.

§ 6. Such are the determining factors in the iron and steel situation in this country. All these factors have cooperated to produce concentration of production. They have been potent influences in promoting or facilitating the development of the Steel Corporation, and to-day are helping to fix its character and operations. Other conditions may have helped toward the same end, but they seem to have been of minor consequence. The railroad rebate which played such an important rôle in the growth of certain other capitalistic organizations exercised relatively little influence in developing the Steel Corporation and the consolidations out of which it was formed. These steel combinations were not due to the absorption by great corporations of smaller rivals which had been brought to terms by means of railroad discriminations, local underselling, and the like. They were unions of various establishments upon a certain plane of business equality formed for increasing productive efficiency or for controlling the market in their several lines of manufacture.

The iron and steel situation in the United States with its tendency toward concentration must be ascribed to the factors which have already been considered. The distribution of ore and coal fields made the industry on a large scale in this country possible and to a considerable extent facilitated consolidation. The growth toward concentra-

tion was greatly influenced by the superior efficiency of
large over small capital, which tended to limit the number
of producers to large corporations, and by the protective
tariff which put foreign manufacturers at a disadvantage in
the home market. The fluctuation of the iron and steel
trade still further accentuated this development by making
the desire to control the industry peculiarly strong.

CHAPTER III

THE BEGINNINGS OF THE UNITED STATES STEEL CORPORATION

§ 1. IN order to explain the nature of the Steel Corporation it will be necessary to devote some space to a discussion of the organizations existing in the North and East which became parts of the corporation at the time of its formation or immediately thereafter. At the beginning of the last decade of the nineteenth century the large iron and steel establishments of the country had come to depend upon the Lake Superior region for most of their ore and upon the coal fields of Pennsylvania for their coke. The introduction of the use of coke and the opening of the ore fields of Michigan and Minnesota had already changed the center of trade activity from the region east of the Alleghanies to that section immediately west. The growth of new markets in the West as well as the relative proximity to the principal ore and coking-coal areas had already made the region in the vicinity of the Great Lakes the great iron and steel producing section of the country. This pre-eminence the district has retained to the present time.

In the same decade the individual and partnership basis of the industry had been supplanted in all the more important concerns by the corporate form of organization. This was due in the main to the growing need of large capital in the equipment of furnaces and mills. At least one organization had already begun the policy of insuring its supply of raw material by securing control of ore and

coal fields.   This policy, afterwards followed by other concerns, necessitated an increasing amount of capital.   As a
natural result the industry was already tending strongly in
the direction of concentration of production.

The period from 1893 to 1897 was one of extreme depression in most branches of manufacture.   It was especially so in the iron and steel trade, where a large number of
establishments went permanently out of business.   It is significant of the tendency toward large-scale production that
of the 123 establishments reported in the Twelfth Census
as abandoned—most of which went out of business during
this critical period—the average capital invested per establishment was only one-fifth that of the organizations
flourishing in 1900.   It was the large concern well equipped
and well situated with respect to ore and coal that was
enabled to survive the crisis of the middle nineties.

§ 2. In 1897 and 1898 the country was recovering from
the severe depression of 1893; and with this recovery the
iron industry awakened to new life.   In much of the industrial field the new era of prosperity was marked by the
formation of great consolidations.   Among the most prominent in the iron and steel trade were the Federal Steel
Company, the American Steel and Wire Company, the
American Tin Plate Company, the National Steel Company, the National Tube Company, the American Steel
Hoop Company, the American Sheet Steel Company, and
the American Bridge Company.   In the Pittsburg region
of Pennsylvania was the Carnegie Company, which, while
not strictly speaking a consolidation, had for several years
past been absorbing a number of establishments, making
it the largest concern of its kind in the world.   All these organizations became parts of the United States Steel Corporation.

With the exception of the Carnegie Company all these

concerns were themselves consolidations of pre-existing corporations. In September, 1898, the Illinois Steel Company, the Minnesota Iron Company, and the Elgin, Joliet, and Eastern Railroad Company were combined to form the Federal Steel Company with an authorized capital of $200,-000,000, of which only $99,743,900 were ever issued.[1] Shortly after the Lorain Steel Company of Ohio and the Lorain Steel Company of Pennsylvania were added to this combination. On December 14, 1898, the American Tin Plate Company was organized with an authorized capital of $50,000,000, of which $46,325,000 were issued. This consolidation, as has been seen, embraced about forty companies and some two hundred and sixty-five mills, producing about ninety-five per cent of the total production of the country.[2] The American Steel and Wire Company, incorporated under the laws of New Jersey, followed on January 13, 1899. This company was successor to the American Steel and Wire Company of Illinois, formed in March of the preceding year.[3] At the time of its formation, it virtually controlled the production of wire goods in this country. Its capital was $90,000,000, all of which was issued. The National Tube and National Steel companies were both organized in February, 1899. The former was capitalized at $80,000,000, and the latter at $59,000,000. The National Tube Company included over a dozen companies. At the time of its organization, it was the largest concern of its kind in the world, and the third largest enaged in the iron and steel business—the Carnegie Company and the Krupps of Germany, alone being larger.[4]

[1] *Commercial and Financial Chronicle*, Sept. 18, 1898, p. 530. *Iron Age*, Sept. 15, 1898.

[2] *Iron Age*, Feb. 16, 1899, p. 17.

[3] *Commercial and Financial Chronicle*, Mar. 12, 1898.

[4] *Ibid.*, July 1, 1899; July 15, 1899.

On April 14, of the same year, the American Steel Hoop Company was formed with a capital of $33,000,000.[1] In March 1900, the American Sheet Steel Company, embracing over a score of companies, was incorporated with an authorized capital of $52,000,000,[2] of which $49,000,000 were issued. In the following month the American Bridge Company was formed with an authorized capital of $70,-000,000, of which $61,055,600 were outstanding. This consolidation absorbed twenty-six firms or companies, and at the time of its organization embraced over nine-tenths of the bridge building interests of the country.[3]

These consolidations which have just been described were regarded as industrial experiments. Their capitalizations were based upon the prediction of promoters that they would be successful. As much time would be required for a justification of such predictions, and as serious dangers from the competition of new enterprises threatened these organizations, their stocks sold at low prices. The organizers of these concerns relied upon the returning prosperity of the country and the monopoly which most of these organizations seemed likely to enjoy, for a considerable period at least, in their several lines of trade.

The future plans, moreover, of these corporations were generally far in advance of any early realization. These plans, in at least one instance, were reflected in an excessively large authorized stock. The Federal Steel Company with an authorized capital of $200,000,000—$100,-000,000 preferred, and $100,000,000 common—had by October, 1899 issued only $53,000,000 preferred and $46,-000,000 common.[4] The American Sheet Steel Company, too, held a considerable portion of its stock in reserve.[5]

[1] *Iron Age*, Oct. 19, 1899.   [2] *Ibid.*, Apr. 5, 1900.
[3] *Ibid.*, May 17, 1900.   [4] *Ibid.*, Oct. 26, 1899.
[5] *Ibid.*, Apr. 5 and May 29, 1900.

§ 3. With extensive plans for future growth and apparently bright prospects for the immediate future, the tendency toward over-capitalization was marked. A large proportion of the issued stock was without any tangible basis. It was determined mainly by possible future gains. According to testimony before the Federal Industrial Commission, the book value of the constituent companies of the Federal Steel Company was placed by experts at $45,000,-000, to which, however, should be added $10,000,000 cash and the value of certain ore and coal properties.[1] According to Mr. Graham, a director of the American Tin Plate Company, only $18,000,000—the amount of the preferred stock—represented the actual value of the mills of the company.[2]

The iron and steel consolidations of 1898-1900 thus tended toward over-capitalization. In this respect they resembled the early period of railroad financiering. There was, however, one important difference: a large part of the capital of railroads has always been represented by bonds, while the industrials which we have just been considering had but little bonded indebtedness. Both had eventually to pass their dividends; but the railroads unable to pay interest on their bonds went into receivers' hands.

The period embraced between the last half of 1898 and the first half of 1900 was an epoch of great prosperity in the iron and steel industry. During this prosperous period the steel combinations followed a policy which threatened their ruin. In an industry subject to such extreme variations in the volume of trade it is wise to build up a substantial reserve during a period of prosperity. It is only by such a policy that the securities of new iron and steel

---

[1] *Iron Age*, Oct. 26, 1899, p. 35.
[2] *Rep. Industrial Commission*, vol. i and vol. xiii, p. 517.

consolidations can eventually be brought up to an investment level. Organized as these new combinations were, the pursuance of such a course would necessitate the passing of dividends. This policy would temporarily lower the market value of their securities and render their sale more difficult; but the corporations would unquestionably have been strengthened.

The interests in control of these various combinations failed to follow this conservative policy; and all of the companies paid regular dividends on their preferred stock from the dates of their organization to January, 1901. The Federal Steel, the American Steel and Wire, and the National Tube companies paid in addition good returns on their common stocks. The total dividends of the Federal Steel, the American Steel and Wire, the National Tube, the National Steel, the American Tin Plate, and the American Steel Hoop companies from their several dates of organization to January 1, 1901 were approximately $30,000,000. Their aggregate capital amounted to over $408,000,000. Their bonded debts were $31,341,271. The surplus reserves at the close of 1900 aggregated $32,687,250, or seven per cent of the total capitalization.[1] When it is remembered that the preferred stock of these combinations represented about the capitalized value of the average earning power of the constituent plants in their separation, and that the common stock represented real or supposed monopoly advantages, economies due to combination, and such working capital as was provided by underwriters, and that fifty-three per cent of the total stock capitalization of the six consolidations already named consisted of common stock whose value could not yet be demonstrated, it is seen that the financial position of these steel concerns after two

[1] *Iron Age Supplement.* Dec. 27, 1900.

years of high prices and large profits was scarcely better than at the outset of their careers.

With this exception the business of these organizations seems to have been ably and honestly conducted. Many improvements were made in their several properties and considerable economies effected. The policy of management in almost every direction was a distinct advance over former methods of trade. However, the lack of ample reserves unfitted these consolidations to withstand trade depression and serious competition. Such depression and threatening competition confronted them in the latter half of 1900.

§ 4. Before discussing the nature of this competition, it will be necessary to describe the business of the Carnegie Steel Company. In the Pittsburg district this organization had, during a period of four decades, grown from a small firm managed by the Kloman Brothers into a concern which owned the most complete and best managed steel plant in the world.[1] The change from the use of anthracite coal to that of coke in the manufacture of iron and steel had given the Pittsburg region peculiar advantages in the matter of assembling material. The region, furthermore, was not far from the best markets. The mills of the Carnegie Company had also been well concentrated; and this fact gave them a pronounced advantage over the companies we have already considered whose mills were generally quite widely scattered. Nor did the advantage of the Carnegie Company stop here. As a result of a policy of large expenditure upon betterments persistently pursued for a number of years, the average excellence of its equipment was far above that of any of its rivals. "Every new pro-

[1] For an interesting, though one-sided, account of the Carnegie Company, see Bridge's *Inside History of the Carnegie Steel Company.*

cess and every new machine which would in any way increase the efficiency, reduce the cost, and improve the products of the Carnegie Company has been adopted, until
this great concern has raised the physical condition of its
mills to a point which is unsurpassed." [1]

The labor force of the company was also strained to the
utmost. Trade unions were banished in 1892, and workmen were encouraged to utmost exertion by high wages
and the promise of advancement. Official rank was strictly
the reward of merit. Every head of a department had an
interest in the business apart from his salary.[2] Every visi-
tor was impressed by the intensity of effort displayed by
the workers in each department. It has been said that the
terrific speed made break-downs frequent at thirty-five, and
old age common at forty-five.

In the early eighties the Carnegie Company—or rather
the Carnegie, Phipps and Company, as it was then called
—had begun the policy which eventually issued in the control of all the factors contributing to the production of steel,
—from the ore and coal in the mine to steel billets and steel
rails. A controlling interest in the stock of the H. C. Frick
Coke Company, the largest owner of coal land in the Connellsville region was secured. This insured the Carnegie
Company not only a majority share in the earnings from
the sale of coke and coal, but also a supply of coke at
prices very close to the cost of production. Notwithstanding Mr. Carnegie's repeated assertion that the best way
to obtain ore is to buy it in the open market, [3] ore supplies
with accompanying transportation facilities were also obtained. In 1896 a five-sixths interest in the stock of the

[1] U. S. *Investor*, Feb. 9, 1901.
[2] See Schwab's testimony, *Report of Industrial Commission*, vol. 13.
[3] Bridge's *Inside History*.

Oliver Iron Mining Company was purchased; and this purchase secured for the Carnegie Company large ore deposits in the Gogebic and the Mesaba ranges. By a fifty year contract with the Rockefeller iron, mining, and transportation companies 1,500,000 tons of soft ore were supplied and transported to the lower lake ports annually. Thus an abundant supply of hard and soft ore at stable and cheap prices was secured. Controlling interests were also obtained in the Pittsburg Steamship Company, which owned, in 1900, eleven steamships and two tug boats, with six additional steamers under construction, and the Pittsburg, Bessemer and Lake Erie Railroad extending from Conneaut, Ohio, to the Carnegie mills at Duquesne. By the close of 1897, the Carnegie Company was almost self-sufficient in all the factors of production. The profits which other steel companies were then adding to their costs, this concern was adding to its earnings.

The example of the Carnegie Steel Company was not lost in the consolidations formed in 1898-1900. The Federal Steel Company, through the Minnesota Iron Company, came into control of large supplies of ore. The company also acquired a considerable acreage of coal land, and aimed to secure adequate means of transportation for the assembling of material. The National Steel Company in like manner obtained control of the sources of some of its ore and coal supply. Indeed, it may be said that all the consolidations of the period were organized with a view of becoming ultimately self-sufficient.

§ 5. Though organized and largely capitalized with such a purpose in view, the manufacturing companies which became constituent parts of the United States Steel Corporation at its beginning were, nevertheless, largely dependent upon one another. The companies may be divided on the basis of their principal products into two classes, the

Carnegie, Federal Steel, and National Steel companies were largely producers of steel billets, ingots, bars, plates. and slabs, materials not in their final form. The National Tube, American Steel and Wire, American Tin Plate, American Steel Hoop, and American Sheet Steel corporations were, as their titles indicate, producers of finished steel goods. These latter companies obtained most of their materials from the primary producers of steel, and converted them into wire, pipes, tin plates, sheets, structural material and the like.

These two groups of companies from their location and the nature of their products had extensive dealings with each other. The western plants of the American Steel and Wire Company and the Ohio plants of the National Tube and American Bridge companies were supplied with wire rods and steel billets by the Federal Steel Company, whose principal plants were located at Chicago. The National Steel Company supplied a portion of the demands of the Tin Plate, Sheet Steel, and Steel Hoop companies, whose financial control was identical with its own. The Carnegie Steel Company furnished material for the finishing mills of the Pittsburg district including representatives from all the companies of the second group.

So long as the various companies confined their trade to certain fields of the iron industry and to certain territories, the harmony of their interests was not seriously disturbed. However, as has been indicated, all these organizations aimed to be ultimately self-sufficient. When the primary producers were about to enter the lines of finished material or the producers of finished material attempted to become independent by invading the fields of those who supplied them with pig iron and steel, a serious competition threatened their financial standing. Being large producers. the successful invasion by any one of the companies of a field hitherto controlled by the others, meant serious injury, if not absolute ruin, to the original occupants.

§ 6. From the winter of 1898-99 to the spring of 1900 prosperity reigned in the steel industry. By the middle of 1900 a reaction in the steel market had set in; and it became evident that trade must adjust itself to a smaller margin of profits. If dividends were to be continued during the periods of reduced demand, every effort must be made to reduce expenses. In no other way could the companies engaged in the manufacture of finished material accomplish this than by securing the largest measure of independence in the field of raw material.

The depression of 1900 hastened the movement towards ultimate independence. The American Steel and Wire Company, a large customer of the Carnegie concern in the Pittsburg region and of the Federal Steel Company in the West, had already acquired two thousand acres of Connellsville coal, and also ore properties with an annual output of 916,000 tons. A fleet of twelve steamers had been acquired from the American Steamship Company. A large steel plant at Milwaukee which would supply raw material to the company's western mills was projected, and in the Pittsburg district there was begun the installation of a complete system of production from ore and coke to wire, wire nails, and springs.[1]

The National Tube Company adopted a similar policy. In the fall of 1900 it began the construction of a large open-hearth steel plant at Wheeling, West Virginia, designed to supply steel billets to all its plants in the Central West. The company, though owning no coal or ore, relied upon its friendly relations with the Federal Steel Company to secure its ore and coal on favorable terms.

[1] *Iron Age*, Dec. 21, 1899.

The National Steel Company which had hitherto relied very largely upon outside corporations for its supply of iron ore and coal now greatly increased its holdings of ore and coal properties. It purchased iron mines with an annual output of 1,300,000 tons and considerable tracts of coal land in the Connellsville and adjoining districts. It also began the installation of a furnace capacity sufficient to supply the total requirements of the Tin-plate, Sheet Steel, and Steel Hoop companies, whose financial control, represented by William & J. H. Moore, was identical with its own.[1]

These threatening movements toward industrial independence led to counter movements on the part of the two chief primary companies. The Federal Steel Company threa' ned to build wire mills unless the American Steel an' Wire Company should abandon the plan of producing its own raw material and renew its wire-rod contract with the Federal Steel Company. As there was nothing to be gained for the present from such a competition, the Steel and Wire Company abandoned its western extensions. In the Pittsburg district, the Carnegie Company began to expand in a similar fashion. In January, 1901, it was announced that the company would construct a large tube mill at Conneaut, Ohio, sheet mills at Homestead, and mills for other finished products in the Pittsburg region. At the same time the Carnegie Company was preparing to secure an independent railroad to the sea-board.

These proposed movements caused serious anxiety to the leaders of the consolidations of the Middle West. In the Pittsburg district, the four Moore companies, the National Tube Company and the eastern trade of the American Steel and Wire Company were threatened by the

[1] *Iron Age*, Dec. 28, 1899; Jan. 4, 1900.

Carnegie organization; and in the Chicago region, the Federal Steel and American Steel and Wire companies were naturally uneasy.

The results of this threatened competition would obviously be ruinous to most of the concerns involved. Heavily over-capitalized, as most of the companies were, and fortified by very inadequate reserves, such competition would mean decreasing profits and the passing of dividends. As a consequence of this there would be a heavy fall in the value of steel stocks. Industrial warfare, too, demands new appliances, and these could only be secured by issuing bonds or by increasing the floating debt. The interests in control of the consolidations strove in every way to avert the impending calamity. Coupled with these interests were the interests of underwriters and promoters who still held large amounts of stock which they had been unable to sell to the public, and thus to reap the large profits upon which they had counted. The decline in the value of these securities, owing to the temporary reaction in the steel trade, made their sale still more difficult in the face of a competition which threatened to overwhelm the new companies. The promoters, underwriters, and original owners of the plants, therefore, were all vitally interested in preventing a break in the harmony of the various steel interests.

§ 7. After the election of 1900, the tide again turned in favor of steel. Everything pointed to an upward movement in steel stocks [1] if the threatened competition among the new consolidations could be averted. Failure to come to some harmonious arrangement would issue in severe loss, and in addition, lock up cash resources at a time when

---

[1] See quotations of steel stocks in *Commercial and Financial Chronicle* during October, November and December, 1900, and January and February, 1901.

projects of new consolidations promised large profits. The
emergency was, therefore, a financial, as well as an industrial, one. The controlling interests in the steel trusts
wished to protect their own holdings; while the promoters
and underwriters not only desired to sell theirs at a good
margin of profit, but also to retain their prestige with the
speculative public. To do this they must prevent a general decline in stock values and avert the impending steel
war.

The course to be adopted by the interests involved was
necessarily one which must not be construed as a reflection
upon their credit. The Carnegie Company was unquestionably the most powerful of the organizations which we
have considered, and the one least likely to be seriously in-
jured by the threatened rivalry. The other corporations
might have surrendered to it; but such a course would
have been a serious compromise of all plans for industrial independence, upon the attainment of which their
capitalizations had been in part based. The course adopted
was a plan by which all the conflicting interests were
united into one corporation organized to own at least a
majority interest in the various steel companies which it
was necessary to control. In this way would competition
be removed. This movement received the backing of the
strongest financial houses in the United States. Mr.
Morgan and his friends, who had been instrumental in the
formation of several of the trusts of the West, now did all
in their power to avert the disaster threatened by the steel
war, and to further the harmony of interests which was
achieved in the formation of the United States Steel Corporation.

The plan to combine embraced at first only four companies—the Carnegie, the Federal Steel, the National Tube,
and the American Steel and Wire. It was principally over

these organizations that the threatened competition was impending. A quick survey of the field, however, showed at least four other concerns which might offer inconveniently active competition, but which could easily be persuaded to enter the confederation. These organizations were the National Steel, the American Tin Plate, the American Steel Hoop, and the American Sheet Steel companies. An attempt was made to purchase the Jones and Laughlin plant at Pittsburg for $30,000,000, but the offer was refused. The Rockefeller ore properties in the Lake Superior region were secured by the payment of $80,000,000 of stock—$40,000,000 preferred, and $40,000,000 common; and the ore carrying fleet was purchased for eight and one-half millions cash. This purchase gave to the new corporation about two-fifths of its ore and nearly one-half of its ore fleet.

The Steel Corporation was organized on February 23, 1901, under the laws of New Jersey with a capital of $3000. This nominal capital was shortly afterwards increased to $1,100,000,000, of which authorized capital stock, $550,000,000 was to be preferred, and $550,000,000 common. The charter gives the corporation the right to increase its preferred and common stock " in such amounts and proportions as shall be determined by the Board of Directors, and as may be permitted by law." [1] The holders of preferred stock are entitled, " to receive when, and as declared, from the surplus or net profits of the corporation yearly dividends at the rate of seven per cent per annum and no more, payable quarterly on dates to be fixed by the by-laws." The cumulative feature of the preferred stock was also guaranteed to the holder in the charter.

[1] *Charter* of U. S. Steel Corporation.   See also *Iron Age*, Feb. 28, 1901, p. 25.

When all cumulative dividends are paid, dividends may be declared on the common stock.

The United States Steel Corporation bought the stock of its constituent companies and controls these organizations by virtue of being the single stockholder in each case. As has already been indicated the companies which became the first members of this consolidation were the Carnegie Steel Company, the Federal Steel Company, the American Steel and Wire Company, the National Tube Company, the National Steel Company, the American Tin Plate Company, the American Steel Hoop Company, and the American Sheet Steel Company. Shortly after its formation the American Bridge Company and the Lake Superior Consolidated Iron Mines entered the organization.

The Lake Superior Consolidated Iron Mines had been incorporated under the laws of New Jersey in 1893. Its purpose was to acquire and operate iron mines in the Mesaba Range, Minnesota. It owned valuable ore properties in the Lake Superior region, some of which it leased to the Carnegie and other steel companies. It owned the Duluth, Mesaba, and Northern Railway, extending from Duluth to Iron Mountain, Minnesota. Its authorized capital was $30,000,000, of which $28,722,000 had been issued at the time of the organization of the Steel Corporation.

§ 8. The exchange of securities between the Steel Corporation and the various constituent companies was affected in such a manner as to afford a bonus to most of the latter. Leaving out of account the Carnegie Steel Company, the aggregate capitalization of the original concerns entering the new organization was $457,070,200. On becoming subsidiary members of the Steel Corporation, this capitalization was raised to $531,914,300, an increase of nearly $75,000,000.

Concerning the ratio of exchange for the securities of the

Carnegie Steel Company no definite official statement has been published, although reports have been made which are apparently authentic. Mr. Morgan in an official announcement declared that $304,000,000 of first mortgage bonds were issued to the holders of Carnegie bonds and sixty per cent of the company's stock.[1] The bonds are reported to have been exchanged at par; and it is further stated that for each $1,000 of Carnegie stock $1500 of first mortgage bonds of the new corporation were issued. As the capital stock of the Carnegie Steel Company in 1901 was $160,000,000, and as these exchanges exactly fit Mr. Morgan's figures, these proportions are probably correct. The remaining forty per cent of Carnegie stock—$64,000,-000—was exchanged for $98,277,120 in preferred, and $90,279,040 in common stock of the Steel Corporation.[2] The entire Carnegie holdings were thus purchased for $492,556,160 par value of stocks and bonds.

§ 9. Mr. Carnegie's personal share in this amount was paid entirely in bonds. Concerning his holdings, Mr. Bridge says, "At the time of the transfer of the Carnegie properties to the United States Steel Corporation, Mr. Carnegie personally held $88,147,000 of the Carnegie Company's bonds. These were exchanged for the Steel Company's bonds at par. He had also 86,382 shares of stock, for which he was paid in bonds at the rate of $1500.00 a share. He therefore acquired $217,720,000 of the bonds of the United States Steel Corporation."[3] If Mr. Bridge's statement is correct, Mr. Carnegie held only a little over half of the bonds of his company and received for his stock

[1] Circular of J. P. Morgan, March 2, 1901.

[2] Bridge, *Inside History of Carnegie Steel Co.*

[3] *Commercial and Financial Chronicle*, Nov. 21, 1903, p. 2039. See also list of stock and bond holders in Bridge's *Inside History of the Carnegie Steel Company*, 4th edition, pp. 356-7.

$129,537,000. Had he owned sixty per cent of the stock, as currently reported, he would have received $144,000,000.

§ 10. The total issues of stock for the Steel Corporation were put in Mr. Morgan's circular of March 2, 1901, at $425,000,000 of seven per cent cumulative preferred and $425,000,000 of common. The new organization thus started on its career with a stock capital of $950,000,000, which, however, was soon increased to over $1,000,000,000. The bonded indebtedness of the Steel Corporation included the $304,000,000 [1] held by the Carnegie interests and some tens of millions of bonded obligations incurred by the constituent companies and assumed by the new consolidation. In addition to these obligations were various mortgage and money liabilities of the constituent companies. At the time the first annual report was issued the total capital as expressed in stocks, bonds, and other liabilities was as follows: [2]

Capital stock—
Preferred...................................... $510,281,100.00
Common....................................... 508,302,500.00

Total capital stock....................... $1,018,583,600.00
Capital stocks of subsidiary companies not held by the
U. S. Steel Corporation......................... 215,914.38
Bonded and debenture debt of the U. S. Steel Corporation (U. S. Steel Corporation bonds $303,757,000).. 360,754,326.77
Mortgage and purchase money obligations of subsidiary companies.................................. 9,590,550.60
Current liabilities................................ 49,826,251.78

Total capital and current liabilities.......... $1,438,970,643.53

---

[1] The bonded debt held by the Carnegie interests was slightly less than this amount. Sixty per cent of the stock of the Carnegie Company was acquired but only $159,450,000 of the bonds. Some more Carnegie bonds were later exchanged, but not the full $160,000,000.

[2] *First Annual Report*, Dec. 31, 1902.

The Steel Corporation, as has already been indicated, controls its constituent companies by virtue of its ownership of their stock. Immediately on its formation, it proceeded with the purchase of the securities of the companies to be controlled. By April 2, 1901, the corporation had acquired ninety-eight per cent of all the stock of the original eight companies. A public offer having been made to the shareholders of the American Bridge Company and the Lake Superior Consolidated Iron Mines to exchange their shares for those of the new organization upon terms contained in Mr. Morgan's circular of April 2, practically all the securities of the former company, and eighty-five per cent of the stock of the latter, were acquired. Arrangements were also made for the acquisition of all outstanding interests in the Oliver Iron Mining Company and the Pittsburg Steamship Company not already owned by the Carnegie Steel Company. These exchanges were all virtually completed by the end of April, 1901. In this way the United States Steel Corporation came by stock ownership into direct management of ten corporations which were already among the largest in the world.

CHAPTER IV

THE UNITED STATES STEEL CORPORATION

§ 1. In the short space of a single chapter, it is impossible to give in any detail a history and description of an organization, the mere cataloguing of whose properties would itself fill a fair-sized volume. The Steel Corporation, furthermore, has been described by such writers as Wilgus and Moody,[1] and certain features of its financial policy have been treated by Meade, Ripley and others. Its place in the development of the steel industry of the United States has been discussed by Hermann Levy,[2] who though a foreign observer, has shown keen insight into the tendencies of the steel trade in this country during the last twenty-five years. It will be the purpose of this chapter to consider only the more salient features of the organization and history of the corporation and certain aspects of its financial condition and business standing which are of special interest from an economic point of view.

§ 2. It may be said that the United States Steel Corporation is typical of a tendency among industrial consolidations to bring under one control all the characteristic lines of work related to a general industry. In the charter under

---

[1] Wilgus, *United States Steel Corporation;* Moody, *Truth about the Trusts,* pp. 133-204. For a good, popular account, see R. S. Baker, "What the United States Steel Corporation really is," *McClure's,* vol. 18, pp. 3-13.

[2] Hermann Levy, *Die Stahlindustrie der Vereinigten Staaten von Amerika.*

which it was organized, the purposes of the corporation are declared to be " to manufacture iron, steel, manganese, coke, copper, lumber and other materials, and all or any articles consisting or partly consisting of iron, steel, copper, wood, or other materials, and all or any products thereof," to acquire or lease lands containing these materials; to mine, extract, or remove coal, ores, stone, other minerals, and timber from any lands occupied or owned by the company or any other lands; and to buy and sell articles consisting, or partly consisting, of these materials.[1]   The United States Steel Corporation is thus an organization for the mining, manufacture, and buying and selling of whatever relates to the iron and steel industry.

This development is an outcome of the tendency noted in a previous chapter to integrate the productive forces of an iron and steel concern.   The companies out of which the corporation was formed were in the main producers of certain classes or grades of commodities.   While they aimed ultimately to be self-sufficient—to produce their own raw, crude, and finished material,—their immediate purpose was to control only special branches of the industry.   The Tinplate Company, for example, endeavored to secure a monopoly of tin plate; and the Steel and Wire Company, of wire goods.   The futility of such attempts and the desirability from the standpoint of producers of controlling a trade so exposed to variations of demand for commodities led to the formation of the Steel Corporation, combination of all the principal branches of iron and steel production under one control.   While all monopolistic intentions[2] are disclaimed by the officials of this consolidation, it has already been seen that the combination was formed to avert a threatened competition which would have lessened profits

---

[1] *Charter*, art. iii.   [2] See *Fourth Annual Report*.

in the prosperous period which was coming, and would have proved destructive to several of the companies in a time of depression. The aim, therefore, of the new organization was, in a measure at least, the control of the industry. How far this object can be said to have been achieved will be discussed later. It is to be noted in this connection that the Steel Corporation is largely the result of the natural vicissitudes of the trade and represents an attempt to control those vicissitudes.

The organization by which the operations of the corporation are carried on presents several features of interest and importance. The Steel Corporation is not an operating company, but what is known as a security-holding corporation. The companies which became parts of it did not lose their identity. The Carnegie Steel Company and the National Tube Company are two distinct organizations, though parts of the same general combination. The central or governing corporation controls the subsidiary companies through ownership of their stock. If the officials of a subsidiary organization adopt a business policy in conflict with that of the controlling body, the latter has simply a stockholder's right of removing the officials of such company and electing others more amenable to its purposes. The subsidiary companies retain the management of their various manufacturing plants, and control such operations and policies as are not of common concern. Each company, for example, pursues its own policy in the matter of recognizing labor unions. Wide latitude is allowed in fixing prices of products which vary with the producing company. One company buys of and sells to another; and bargains are driven as shrewdly as ever. In the event of dispute, the executive committee acted, in the first year or two of the corporation's existence, as a sort of supreme court. At the present time conflicting interests between the companies are harmonized by either the advisory or the finance committee.

While each subsidiary company maintains a sort of local or special jurisdiction over its own peculiar operations, those interests common to all or to several of the companies are usually combined in great general departments. The coke interests, the various branches of manufacture, and the like are united in such departments under single heads.   A single agency distributes iron ore, coal, and coke among the various plants.   By this means cross-shipments are avoided; plants are supplied from the nearest sources of supply; and material is sent to those places where it is most needed.   In the matter of prices where two or more companies are concerned, arrangements are made at the conferences of the managers of sales of the subsidiary organizations.   These price arrangements are much influenced by departmental officials and by the business policy of the central governing body.

The Steel Corporation is under the control of a board of twenty-four directors.   The direct management is vested in the chairman of the board of directors, the president, several subordinate officials, the finance committee, and the advisory committee.[1]   All these functionaries are appointed by the board.   The chairman of the board of directors presides at all meetings of the stockholders and of the board, and has general supervision of matters designated to him by the board or finance committee.   The president is the head of the manufacturing side of the corporation's activity, the chairman of the advisory committee, and an *ex-officio* member of the finance committee.   The most important executive body of the organization is the finance committee, consisting of seven members, who as far as prac-

---

[1] By-laws of the U. S. Steel Corporation, arts. iii, iv, v.

ticable, must be persons of experience in matters of finance. This body has special charge and control of all financial affairs of the company; and during the intervals between the meetings of the board of directors it may exercise all the powers of the board. The advisory committee, consisting of three members besides the president of the corporation, is a body with powers to consider such questions relating to manufacturing, transportation, or operation, as may be submitted to the committee by the president.

It is significant of the general policy of the Steel Corporation that the ruling power is financial. The leading executive body is the finance committee; and the president, who is at the head of the industrial side of the organization, is subordinate in managerial power to the chairman of the board and the chairman of the finance committee. The board of directors, too, is composed mainly of financiers. When the corporation was first organized only about one-third of the board were acquainted with the language of steel.[1] The banking interests were represented by J. P. Morgan, Geo. C. Perkins, and Robert Bacon; the Standard Oil, by the Rockefellers and H. H. Rogers. The Steel Corporation, therefore, has been at least as much a financial as a manufacturing organization. Most of the business and industrial policy of the consolidation is determined by meetings of the heads of departments and various committees.[2] Mr. Bridge, in his *Inside History of the*

---

[1] The directors in 1901 were J. P. Morgan, J. D. Rockefeller, H. H. Rogers, Chas. M. Schwab, Elbert H. Gary, Geo. C. Perkins, E. C. Converse, Jas. Gayley, Marshall Field, D. G. Reid, J. D. Rockefeller, Jr., A. Gifford, Robt. Bacon, Nathaniel Thayer, Abram Hewitt, C. S. Griscom, F. H. Peabody, Chas. Steele, W. H. Moore, N. B. Ream, P. A. B. Widener, J. H. Reed, H. C. Frick, and Wm. Edenborn. *Cf. First Annual Report.*

[2] *First Annual Report,* p. 21.

Carnegie Steel Company graphically describes the weekly meetings of the board of managers, superintendents, assistants, etc., of that company. Meetings of a somewhat similar nature are periodically held by the officials of the larger organization. Friendly rivalries are encouraged. Inventions and improved processes are made the common property of all the plants which can use them; and all information concerning trade policy is discussed in common by representatives of the plants concerned.

§ 3. By the formation of the Steel Corporation two hundred and thirteen different manufacturing plants and transportation companies, forty-one mines, nearly one thousand miles of railroad connecting ore, coke, and manufacturing properties, and a lake fleet of one hundred and twelve vessels constituting about one-third of the total tonnage of the Northern Lakes were united under one controlling interest.[1] Of the manufacturing plants, one hundred were in Pennsylvania; fifty-one in Ohio; fifteen in Illinois; twelve in Indiana; twelve in New York; and the rest scattered from Connecticut to California. The company also controlled seventy-eight blast furnaces,[2] more than one-third of the entire number in the United States. Several of these furnaces have a daily capacity of seven hundred tons.

The coking-coal properties of the Steel Corporation, upon whose value Mr. Schwab placed such emphasis in his testimony before the Industrial Commission,[3] comprised some 57,000 acres located in Westmoreland and Fayette Counties, Pennsylvania. This area constitutes part of the famous Connellsville region. In the fall of 1901 considerable additions to this area were made in Pennsylvania; and the

---

[1] *Report of Industrial Commission,* vol. xiii, p. 471.

[2] *Commercial and Financial Chronicle,* Apr. 27, 1901, p. 171.

[3] *Report,* vol. xiii, pp. 464, 467, 472.

lease of 50,000 acres of the Pocahontas district in West Virginia was effected. Besides these properties in coking-coal a considerable area of steam and gas coal in Illinois came into the possession of the corporation.

The most important asset of the Steel Corporation has been its valuable mines of iron ore in Minnesota, Michigan, and Wisconsin. This region is generally divided into five " ranges ": the Menominee and Marquette, in Michigan; the Gogebic, partly in Michigan and partly in Wisconsin; and the Vermillion and Mesaba, in Minnesota.[1] All these ranges are within two hundred miles of the shores of Lake Superior. At the time of the organization of the United States Steel Corporation, the Vermillion range produced approximately 1,700,000 tons of ore annually, nearly all of which belonged to the new corporation; the Gogebic range, 2,800,000 tons, 1,700,000 of which came under the control of the new organization; the Menominee, 3,100,000 tons, of which the Steel Corporation controlled 2,000,000; the Marquette, 3,300,000 tons of which 1,400,000 belonged to the same organization; and of the 7,800,000 tons produced in the Mesaba range, the corporation would have 5,700,000 tons.[2]

Just what proportion of the Lake Superior ore fields came into the possession of the Steel Corporation is difficult to state, and has been variously estimated. At the end of the year 1902, when the first annual report of the Steel Corporation came out, it had shipped during that year over sixty per cent of all the ore production of the Lake Superior region, and controlled about forty-five per cent of the entire

[1] See *Ore Deposits of U. S. and Canada,* by J. F. Kemp, Scientific Publishing Co.; also Mussey, *Combination in the Mining Industry,* in Columbia University *Series in History, Economics and Public Law.*

[2] *Age of Steel,* Jan., 1901, p. 115; April 20, 1901. *Iron Age,* Feb. 21. 1901.

output of the country. Its proportion of the entire supply of workable ore in the ground has been placed very high. Mr. Schwab in his statement before the Industrial Commission estimated this proportion at not less than eighty per cent of the total deposits of the Lake Superior district. The ore fields of the Carnegie, Federal Steel, National Steel, and American Steel and Wire companies, were estimated to contain at least 500,000,000 tons.[1] In addition to this the Rockefeller holdings were supposed to represent about one-half the iron ore of the Mesaba range, or approximately 250,000,000.[2] If these estimates were correct the Steel Corporation would have come into possession of 750,000,-000 tons of workable ore.

The estimates may have been exaggerated as any calculation of the amount of available ore in a district can at best only approximate the truth. What proportion of the ore fields came under the control of the corporation is hard to determine. The Hill holdings in the Mesaba Range which the Steel Corporation recently leased have been estimated to contain as much as 500,000,000 tons. Several independent companies have additional holdings. In view of these facts the Steel Corporation probably came into possession of not more than half the deposits of the Lake Superior district.

In 1901, however, much of this region was imperfectly known; and hence the holdings of the new steel consolidation were over-estimated. In view of the current opinion of the time, we can readily appreciate the feeling voiced by the New York *Independent*:

It is quite plain that the corporation will soon own nearly all

[1] *Report of Industrial Commission*, vol. 1, p. 1023.

[2] *Age of Steel*, Mar. 23, 1901, p. 15. *Review of Reviews*, May, 1901, p. 560.

the northern ore supply. Its control is already so well established that the annual meeting of the ore-producers to make prices for the season has been postponed indefinitely, because prices will be determined by the corporation. This gathering-in of the iron mines by the new combination is a movement of great importance. It will make the corporation absolute master of the American iron and steel industry.[1]

While occupying a commanding position among iron and steel producers, the Steel Corporation did not monopolize the Lake Superior region. Nevertheless, it did obtain possession of much of the best ore regions in the world. But as the later history of the Lake Superior region has shown, independent companies have pre-empted large sections of this valuable district. No sooner was the Steel Corporation organized than several companies, alive to their own interests, secured possession or leases of property in these fields. Among the most active was Mr. J. J. Hill, whose ore lands became nearly as extensive as those of the Steel Corporation itself, and whose railroad interests helped to make him one of its most formidable rivals.[2]

§ 4. During the six years of its existence, the Steel Corporation has maintained the same general features which characterized it at the outset of its career. It has, however, extended its control over some large independent concerns, and added to its holdings of coal and ore land; it has reorganized some of the constituent companies; it has transferred much of its preferred stock into a bonded indebtedness; it has introduced a novel scheme of profit-sharing; and it has shown some interesting vicissitudes in its earnings and in its relative share of the country's iron and steel trade.

[1] New York *Independent*, April 11, 1901, p. 862.
[2] See *Iron Trade Review*, Feb. 19, 1903.

Among the most notable additions to the Steel Corporation since its organization have been the Shelby Steel Tube Company in 1901; the Union Steel Company in December, 1902; the Troy Steel Products Company in January, 1903; the holdings of the Chemung Iron Company of Duluth in August, 1903; the properties of the Clairton Steel Company in May, 1904; and the lease of the Hill holdings in the Lake Superior region in October, 1906.

The Shelby Steel Tube Company, which became a part of the corporation about the time that the exchange of shares had been effected with the American Bridge Company and the Lake Superior Consolidated Iron Mines, was the largest maker of seamless tube in the world.[1] This organization, however, had been greatly overcapitalized. The basis of exchange of shares was $37.50 of the corporation's preferred for $100.00 of Shelby Steel Tube preferred, and $25.00 of the corporation's common for $100.00 of Shelby Steel Tube common.

The Union Steel and Troy Steel Products companies were added in 1902 and 1903.[2] The former organization had absorbed seven other companies and had a controlling interest in two others. Its bonds, amounting to $45,000,000, were guaranteed by the Steel Corporation. The Troy Steel Products Company was a much smaller concern, and the entire issues of capital stock and first mortgage bonds were purchased for $1,100,000.

The purchase of the holdings of the Chemung Iron Company of Duluth added some extensive and valuable fields of iron ore. By this purchase there was acquired what the *Iron Age* describes as "the last really large and important block of Mesaba ore that was for sale." These holdings

[1] *Age of Steel*, June 29, 1905, p. 15.
[2] *First Annual Report*, Dec. 31, 1902.

are said to include " eleven more or less fully developed and
as yet entirely unmined tracts, in all about 70,000,000 tons
of ore of excellent quality, much of it of high grade Bessemer, much of it cheaply mined and readily reducible. The
lands are mostly leased properties on a basis of twenty-five
cents a ton royalty." [1]

The Clairton Steel properties consisted mainly of a large
manufacturing plant at Clairton, Pennsylvania, 2644 acres
of coking-coal land in Fayette County of the same state,
20,000 acres in fee of mineral lands on the Marquette range,
and considerable railroad and limestone property.[2] Of the
bonded debt carried by the Clairton Steel Company, $10,-
230,000 were guaranteed by the United States Steel Corporation, the remainder being mortgages on property in
which the corporation had a part interest. In consideration for the transfer of the company's stock, there was
paid to the vendors $1,000,000 par value of the United
States Steel Corporation 10-60 year five per cent bonds.

The transfer of the Hill holdings in October, 1906, has
excited much attention as indicative of the policy of the
corporation to control the northern ore supply. The conditions of this transfer are stated in the following announcement made by Judge E. H. Gary, Chairman of the Board
of Directors of the Steel Corporation:

After long negotiations, a contract has been signed for the
acquisition on a royalty basis of the Hill ore properties (so-
called) by companies controlled by the United States Steel
Corporation. The quantity of the ore has not been accurately
determined, but it is a large body. The price to be paid is
$1.65 per ton, delivered at the upper lake docks, with an in-
crease of 3.4 cents per ton each succeeding year. The mini-

[1] *Commercial and Financial Chronicle*, Aug. 22, 1903, p. 405.

[2] *Third Annual Report*. Also *Iron and Steel Directory*, 1904, pp.
70-71.

mum agreed to be mined is 750,000 tons for the year 1907, and increases of 750,000 tons per year until it reaches 8,250,000 tons, and thereafter it continues on that basis. It is believed that the consummation of this agreement will result in great benefit to both parties.[1]

In considering this notable addition to the ore lands owned or controlled by the Steel Corporation two questions naturally suggest themselves: What will be its effect upon the corporation itself? What will be its consequences to the iron trade at large? In securing the most extensive deposits of Lake Superior ore held by a single interest apart from itself, it has made an important addition to the number of years of operation guaranteed to its blast furnaces and mills by the lake ores it previously controlled. It is probably assured of supplies outlasting by a great many years those of its principal competitors. It must be said, however, that it has paid no small price to the Great Northern for the privilege of taking all the ore the latter has to offer. And furthermore, the transaction by increasing the cost of producing ore to the Steel Corporation has improved the position of some of its competitors.

The effect on the iron and steel trade as a whole is likely to show itself in a general marking up of ore values. The position of the Southern producers of foundry and basic irons in competition with the merchant furnaces of the East and the Central West will doubtless be advanced. Eastern producers are likely to have an additional incentive for the use of foreign ores, and in some regions for the development of deposits at home.

While the transfer of these properties is significant, it should be clearly stated that the Hill holdings leased to the Steel Corporation do not include the developed mines owned

[1] *Iron Age*, Oct. 11, 1906, p. 953.

by the Great Northern interests.   Such noted mines as the
Mahoning, Stevenson, and others, Mr. Hill could not con-
vey.   With the exception of two newly opened mines no
actual mining operations have been conducted on the lands
leased.   A considerable part of them has been thoroughly
explored.   It is said that 100,000,000 tons of ore are in
sight on the property leased; but as much of these fields
have not been tested, the actual tonnage is probably very
much more,[1] the estimates ranging from 300,000,000 to
500,000,000 tons.

The acquisition of the Hill properties is in line with the
policy which the corporation has pursued since its organization.   The Union Steel Company and the Clairton Steel
Company on entering this consolidation added large areas
of ore land.   The purchase of the holdings of the Chemung
Iron Company of Duluth and what is known as the Canisteo
deal late in 1905 took into the Steel Corporation ownership
more than 200,000,000 tons of ore.[2]   All these additions
show that the growth of the company's control over the
northern ore land has been marked and rapid since its organization in 1901.   What proportion of the Lake Superior ore region is now owned or held by the Steel Corporation is difficult to state; but it seems probable that it
is not less than three-fourths, and may be considerably
more.

§ 5.   While the United States Steel Corporation was extending its control over other companies and properties, it
was also making certain other extensions and internal
changes.   During the first three years of its existence the
export trade was under the supervision of a departmental
head.   During the depression of 1903-4 this trade assumed

[1] *Iron Age*, Oct. 18, 1906, p. 1007.
[2] *Ibid.*

an importance greater than in 1901-2.   Early in 1904 there was organized the United States Steel Products Export Company with general offices in New York City.   " This Company does not manufacture finished or unfinished products of any kind, but has for its object the extension and development of the export trade of the United States Steel Corporation." [1]   As the United States is to-day the largest producer of iron and steel in the world, the export trade of its greatest producer is important to the country.   The direct control of the new company is vested in the Federal Steel Company.

Another development is the organization of the Indiana Steel Company, also to be directly controlled by the Federal Steel Company.   The formation of this concern is due to the rapid growth of the steel trade in the West, and the inability of the mills in Illinois to meet the increased demand for their commodities.   We are told by the officials that :

in consequence of these conditions, it has been decided to construct and put in operation a new plant, to be located on the south shore of Lake Michigan, in Calumet Township, Lake County, Indiana ; and a large acreage of land has been purchased for that purpose.   It is proposed to construct a plant of the most modern standard and to completely equip it for the manufacture of pig iron, Bessemer and open-hearth steel, and a great variety of finished steel products.   The total cost will be large.[2]

It is the purpose of the corporation to make this plant the largest and best equipped of its kind in the world. Furnaces and rolling mills will cover a square mile in ex-

[1] *Iron and Steel Works Directory*, 1904, p. 39.

[2] *Fourth Annual Report*, December, 1905.

tent; and in addition thousands of acres owned by the Indiana Company will be used for a town site. This town, the name of which will be Gary, will form a large industrial community dependent mainly upon the steel plant. The plant, which is to cost $75,000,000, is being built primarily to serve the Western market, but is so located that its product can be marketed advantageously in the East as well as in the West.[1]

§ 6. Coincident with these extensions the constituent companies themselves have undergone some noteworthy changes. In March, 1903, the Carnegie Steel Company of New Jersey came into existence through a combination of the original Carnegie Steel Company of Pennsylvania, the National Steel Company, and the American Steel Hoop Company. The capital stock was fixed at $63,000,000, all of which is common.[2] A similar merger took place in December, 1903, between the American Sheet Steel and the American Tin Plate companies. This combination is now known as the American Sheet and Tin Plate Company.[3] The capital stock is fixed at $49,000,000 of which $24,500,-000 is seven per cent cumulative preferred, and $24,500,000; common. This merger was part of a plan of enforced economy due to the depression of the latter months of 1903.[4] In these months occurred a dismantling of several of the least productive mills and a removal of the headquarters of nearly all the subsidiary companies to Pittsburg.

After these extensions and reorganizations, the United States Steel Corporation may now (March, 1907) be said to control directly the following companies, which in turn control numerous other subsidiary interests:

[1] *Iron Age*, Apr. 26, 1906, p. 1417.
[2] *Iron and Steel Directory*, 1904, p. 3.   [3] *Ibid.*, p. 53.
[4] *Commercial and Financial Chronicle*, Nov. 14, 1903, p. 1877.

Carnegie Steel Company (of New Jersey).
Federal Steel Company.
National Tube Company.
Shelby Steel Tube Company.
American Steel and Wire Company (New Jersey).
American Sheet and Tin Plate Company.
American Bridge Company (New Jersey).
Union Steel Company.
Clairton Steel Company.
Lake Superior Consolidated Iron Mines.

Of these companies, the Steel Corporation owns practically all the stock. It also owns one-sixth of the stock of the Oliver Iron Mining Company and of the Pittsburg Steamship Company, the remaining five-sixths of both being owned by the Carnegie Steel Company. In the Lake Superior region through its subsidiary companies, it owns or has a controlling share in sixty-five active mines,[1] besides extensive fields containing large quantities of ore not yet mined. Its coking-coal area embraces over 113,000 acres, and its tracts of steam coal, over 32,000 acres.[2] It owns over eleven hundred miles of railroad, including branches and spurs, and operates under trackage rights, 297 miles more.[3] Its blast furnaces number ninety-three, and its iron and steel mills over seven hundred.

§ 7. On January 1, 1906, there was a capital stock of $868,583,600 and a bonded indebtedness of $570,472,264-93.[4] Of the capital stock, $508,302,500 is common, and $360,281,100, preferred. At the close of the first year of the corporation's existence the preferred stock amounted to $510,281,100. Its contraction is the outcome of a plan by which $150,000,000 preferred stock was converted into a bonded indebtedness.

---

[1] *Fourth Annual Report.*   [2] *Ibid.*   [3] *Ibid.*   [4] *Ibid.*

§ 8. Of the business policies of the Steel Corporation none has probably excited more attention and received more severe criticism than has this conversion plan proposed in the spring of 1902. Under the date of April 17, the Steel Corporation announced a plan for the exchange of $200,-000,000 of the preferred stock for a like amount of second mortgage collateral trust bonds, and asked the stockholders for authority to create a mortgage on the property, limited to $250,000,000, of which $50,000,000 was to be sold for cash, the remainder being exchanged in the manner above indicated. The announcement created great surprise, especially as the earnings of the previous nine months showed a most surprising surplus. However, at a special meeting, the proposition was voted on and approved by the stockholders representing $374,574,100 par value of the preferred stock and $395,855,700 par value of the common stock. Within a few days of the ratification of the conversion plan, suit was begun by certain owners of stock to prevent the proposed issue of bonds and retirement of preferred stock. An order was granted on June 9, by a New Jersey court to show cause why the corporation should not be restrained from changing stock into bonds. This temporary injunction was made permanent on June 16; and the case was appealed to the Court of Errors and Appeals at Trenton, and awaited its turn on the calendar. On September 26, 1902, the court handed down its decree reversing and disolving the injunction. Other legal complications arose, but the legality of the conversion plan was upheld.

The motives which led to the proposed plan have been a subject of much controversy. The alleged motive of the corporation was the need of money for proposed improvements. It was further urged that the payment of five per cent interest on $250,000,000 of bonds in place of seven per cent dividends on preferred stock of $200,000,000 would result in an annual saving of $1,500,000. In view of the large earnings of 1902 and the early part of 1903, these motives were seriously questioned; and the plan with its provisions for the underwriting syndicate met with such criticism that the arrangement was closed when $150,-000,000 of preferred stock had been exchanged and $20,-000,000 of bonds sold.[1]

§ 9. Another plan of the corporation which excited much comment, favorable and unfavorable, at the time of its first publication was the famous profit-sharing scheme. Under the date of December 31, 1902, two circulars, one addressed to the stockholders and another to the officers and employees, were issued in which a plan was proposed whereby the officers and employees might be given an opportunity to become stockholders. Two million dollars of preferred stock were to be set aside for purchase by employees of the corporation. The stock was to be sold for $82.50 a share, and a bonus of five dollars a share for five years was to be added to the regular seven per cent dividend. The workers were divided into six classes according to annual salary, beginning with those receiving $20,000 or over, who embraced the first class. The sixth class included those receiving $800 or less; the other classes embraced those receiving intermediate amounts. The proportion of stock which could be owned by these several classes varied inversely with their salary. The members of the first class could own stock to an amount not exceeding five per cent of their annual income. The second class was limited to eight per cent of their yearly income; the third class to ten

[1] For a defense of the bond conversion, see editorials in *Commercial and Financial Chronicle* in the summer of 1902. For a criticism, see Meade in *Quarterly Journal of Economics*, vol. 18, p. 22; also Ripley, *Quarterly Journal*, Feb., 1905.

per cent; the fourth to twelve per cent; the fifth to fifteen
per cent; and the sixth to twenty per cent. The object of
the provision was

to interest the large number of young and able employees in
the work of more closely organizing and systematizing the
business in all its branches and ramifications—as an integral
part of the Steel Corporation as an harmonious whole; to interest these men in reducing general expenses as well as the
particular cost of manufacture; to offer to these men an inducement to remain permanently in the Corporation's service;
and to avoid the tendency of a profit-sharing plan pertaining
solely to a constituent company.[1]

To this proposition the Amalgamated Association of
Iron and Steel Workers made no opposition, and a large
number of the employees availed themselves of the opportunity to buy shares. During the period of declining earnings in the latter half of 1903, many of the workmen who
had invested in the shares of the company complained of
the possibility of losing their investments. The corporation then voluntarily promised to buy back in 1908 the
shares of any of its employees who might then wish to sell
and who were still in its employ at the price at which the
shares were purchased. By this agreement, the Steel
Corporation virtually guaranteed the integrity of the workmen's investments.

The setting aside of shares for employees has been repeated each year since the introduction of the plan; and the
conditions of the offer, except in the matter of price, have
been substantially the same. Under the offer made at the
end of 1905, " subscriptions were received from 12,256 employees, for a total of 23,989 shares." [2]   By the close of the

[1] Circular to Stockholders, Dec. 31, 1902.
[2] *Fourth Annual Report,* p. 24.

year 1905, there had been issued to employees of the corporation over 120,000 shares of stock.

The differences in the price paid for stock due to variation in market value from year to year have been a source of some complaint among workmen. The employees who purchased stock at the time of the first offer secured their shares at $82.50 per share; at the end of 1903, the price was fixed at $55.00; a year later, at $87.50; at the end of 1905, at $100.00; and in December, 1906, at $103.00.[1] The workmen, however, in most cases have recognized that these variations are due to market conditions, and that in each case the stock has been offered them at some discount.

This profit-sharing scheme represents an attempt on the part of the company to interest employees in the success of the business by giving them an interest in the profits. In this particular it does not differ essentially from other profit-sharing schemes. Making employees, however, a part of the corporation by making them stockholders, is a departure from the usual forms which profit-sharing plans have assumed in the past. It is not, indeed, the first attempt of the kind ever made. The National Steel Company before becoming a part of the Steel Corporation had persuaded many of its workmen to become investors in its preferred stock, and in the Carnegie Company the policy of giving officials and departmental heads an interest in the business outside of their usual salaries had long been pursued. The scheme, however, is none the less significant. How far it will make employees feel that their interests are identical with those of the corporation remains to be seen, and its outcome promises to be of more than ordinary economic and sociological interest.

§ 10. The earnings of the corporation have exhibited

[1] New York *Evening Sun*, Dec. 14, 1906.

some interesting features both on account of their magnitude and variation. Starting out as the organization did with a capital in round numbers of $1,400,000,000, it was a question whether the earnings would justify this huge capitalization. While it cannot be said that the income has come up to the sanguine expectations of the organizers, the returns have nevertheless been large. It must be remembered, however, that the period since the organization of the company has on the whole been one of great prosperity. The corporation has not yet been compelled to weather a time of depression comparable to that of the middle nineties, and until it has experienced such an epoch, its strength and stability will remain problematical.

While the period since 1901 has been on the whole one of prosperity there has been sufficient variation in trade considerably to affect the income. The total sales of the corporation for 1902, the year for which the first annual report was issued, amounted to $560,510,479. The magnitude of this income will be appreciated when it is remembered that our national revenues for the fiscal year ending June 30, 1905, aggregated $543,423,859, or $17,086,620 less than the gross earnings of the corporation for 1902. During the year 1904 the gross receipts fell to $444,405,-430.56. This decline was due to the depression which set in in the latter part of the year 1903 and lasted through most of 1904. Near the close of the latter year a revival in the iron and steel trade began which has continued to the present time (March, 1907). With this revival the gross receipts of the corporation have greatly increased, those for 1905 being nearly $25,000,000 more than the gross earnings for 1902.

The variation of the trade was more forcibly reflected in the net earnings. Net earnings in the corporation's annual reports signify that part of the total income remaining above cost of manufacture, operating expenses, interest on bonds of subsidiary companies, taxes, and debts incurred for ordinary repairs. Out of the total net earnings are paid the interest on the corporation's bonds, dividends, appropriations for additional properties, extraordinary repairs, and sinking funds. The amount remaining after these obligations have been met constitute the " balance of surplus " for the year; and these surpluses constitute a reserve fund (the undivided surplus).

The total net earnings of the Steel Corporation for the years 1902-1906 [1] with the yearly balances of surplus have been as follows:

	Net Earnings.	Balance of Surplus.
1902	$133,308,763.00	$34,253,656.75
1903	109,171,152.35	12,304,916.59
1904	73,176,521.73	5,047,852.19
1905	119,787,658.43	17,065,815.15
1906	156,624,273.18	12,742,859.94

It will be seen from this table that the banner year of the corporation was 1906. Owing to large appropriations for improvements and extensions the surplus remaining for the corporation's reserve fund is less than half that for 1902, the year of the next largest net earnings.

During the six years of the Steel Corporation's history the net earnings have been sufficient for the payment of the annual dividends of seven per cent on the preferred stock. Down to October, 1903, the annual dividends on the common stock had been four per cent. They were then cut in half; and in April, 1904 they were passed. On July 31, 1906, it was announced that dividends on the common stock would be resumed. Since then quarterly dividends of one half of one per cent have been paid.

[1] *Annual Reports* of the Steel Corporation, and *Iron Age*, Jan. 31, 1907. p. 354.

The net earnings of the corporation have thus fluctuated considerably during the six years of its existence. The company during part of that time has been compelled to forego dividends on much of its stock, and fortify itself against outside competition by making large appropriations for improvements and extensions. This fact indicates that the organization is as yet far from controlling the conditions of iron and steel production. Concerning the depression of three years ago, the Iron Age declares:

It has been truthfully said that in 1904 the United States Steel Corporation passed through the worst year in its history from every standpoint; and this being true of this great interest, it naturally follows that it is also true of all other leading iron and steel concerns. It is a matter of congratulation that the Corporation, in spite of the adverse conditions existing, was able to maintain and pay regular dividends upon its preferred stock and at the same time keep up and improve the physical condition of its plants.

And yet this depression lasted but little over a year and was mild compared with such periods as the middle nineties and the middle seventies. When it is remembered that the iron and steel trade is peculiarly subject to the fluctuations of business and that the company carries a bonded debt of half a billion dollars, it can hardly be said that the financial stability of the Steel Corporation is fully assured.

§ 11. Of allied interest and of even more significance is the corporation's relative share of the country's trade. Perhaps no industrial combination excited such apprehension of monopoly power and tyranny as did this company at the time of its formation.[1] This apprehension is readily accounted for by its great size—its immense capital and large property holdings. While controlling a large share of

[1] For a dark picture of such industrial tyranny, see quotation from London *Standard* in *Iron Age*. Mar. 28. 1901, p. 4.

the country's iron and steel trade, the Steel Corporation exercises no such dominating influence over the industry as do the Standard Oil and American Sugar Refining companies in their respective fields. Nor has its relative share of the country's production tended to increase. Independent concerns have maintained a vigorous activity and have even gained on their great competitor.

When the Steel Corporation was first organized it was estimated that the company's control of the country's output of Bessemer ore would be about ninety per cent,[1] and of the iron ore lying in the ground, fully seventy-five per cent.[2] Wilgus in his work on the United States Steel Corporation stated that it would make eighty per cent of the Bessemer steel; fifty to sixty per cent of the open-hearth; two-thirds of the steel rails made in the United States, Canada, and Mexico; sixty per cent of the steel beams; two-thirds of the wire rods; ninety-four per cent of the wire; ninety-five per cent of the wire nails; all the woven wire and barbwire fence; ninety-five per cent of the steel in tubes; ninety-five per cent of all the tin plate; and ninety per cent of all the bridge material. While some of these estimates approximate the truth, most of them proved extravagant. However, very conservative calculations gave the corporation sixty per cent of the output of pig iron and from eighty to eighty-five per cent of rolled or finished products.

Considering the size of the Steel Corporation, the proportion of its trade has, at no period, been very startling. In 1901, it produced 43.9 per cent of the iron ore of the country, 42.9 per cent of the pig iron, 66.2 per cent of the total steel ingots and castings, and 50.1 per cent of the rolled products. In addition to this it controlled 65.8 per

[1] New York *Independent*, Apr. 11, 1901.
[2] *Review of Reviews*, May, 1901, p. 560.

cent of the output of wire nails.[1]   It may be said, however, that its control of the higher grades of ore, pig iron, and rolled products was larger than these figures would indicate.   Of the 20,589,237 tons of ore shipped from the Lake Superior region, the Steel Corporation shipped 12,692,213 tons, or 61.6 per cent.   It produced 58.5 per cent of the Bessemer and basic pig iron, and 70.2 per cent of the Bessemer steel ingots and castings.   Among rolled products, the corporation produced 59.9 per cent of the Bessemer steel rails; 62.2 per cent of the structural shapes; 64.6 per cent of the plates and sheets; and 77.6 per cent of the wire rods.   Of certain wire goods like woven and barb wire the Steel Corporation had practically a monopoly by virtue of patent rights.

Since 1901 the proportion of the trade controlled by the company has not varied to a very marked extent.   In 1902 the aggregate of that trade was large; but independent concerns secured a due share of it.   The most noteworthy changes were in regard to steel rails which increased from a proportion of 59.9 per cent to 65.4 per cent and wire rods which declined from a percentage of 77.6 to one of 71.5.

The year 1903 marks a relative decline in the proportion of raw and crude material and a slight advance in the percentage of finished and rolled goods.   The increase, however, was followed by a noticeable decline in 1904 and 1905.   The proportion of pig iron and open-hearth steel produced by the corporation has held its own.   With these and a few other exceptions, the company's share of the total production from 1902 to 1905 (inclusive) shows a small but appreciable decline.

The amounts of iron and steel produced by the Steel Corporation and independent concerns for 1905 and the percentages of the total for each year from 1902 to 1905 are shown in the following table: [2]

[1] *Iron Age*, Jan. 2, 1903.   [2] Taken from figures in *Iron Age*.

IMPORTANCE OF THE UNITED STATES STEEL CORPORATION IN PRODUCTION

	By the United States Steel Corporation. (1905)	By independent companies. (1905)	Total shipments and products. (1905)	Percentage produced by the Steel Corporation.			
				1905.	1904.	1903.	1902.
Shipments of ore from Lake Superior—gross tons	19,251,872	15,101,584	34,353,456	56.8	53.8	58.8	60 4
Total production of iron ore—gross tons	18,846,556	24,039,567	42,526,133	43.5	38.0	43.8	45.1
Production of coke—net tons	12,242,909	20,060,297	32,303,206	37.9	36.6	34.2	37.4
Production of iron and steel—gross tons:							
Bessemer, basic, low phosphorus, foundry, and other kinds of pig-iron ...	9,951,891	12,746,513	22,698,404	43.8	44.3	39 9	44.3
Spiegelesen, ferro manganese, ferro-phosphorus, and ferro bessemer	220,257	73,719	293,976	74.9	70.5	81.0	81 0
Total pig iron	10,172,148	12,820,232	22,992,380	44.2	44.6	4C.4	44.7
Bessemer steel ingots and castings	7,379,188	3,562,187	10,941,375	67.4	69.0	72.0	73.9
Open-hearth steel ingots and casings	4,616,051	4,355,325	8,971,376	51.4	50.4	51.0	52.4
Total steel ingots and castings	11,995,239	7,917,512	19,912,751	60.2	61.0	63.5	65.7
Bessemer steel rails	1,713,610	1,478,737	3,192,347	53 6	57.2	C5.6	65.4
Structural shapes	908,C96	752,443	1,660,519	54.6	55.1	60.3	57.9
Plates, sheets, including black plates and excluding nail plat.s	2,028,429	1,503,801	3,532,230	57.4	58.0	59.9	59.4
Wire rods	1,265,707	542,981	1,808,688	69.9	71.3	73.1	71.5
Bars, skelp, nail plates, open-hearth and iron rails, and other finished rolled products	2,063,113	4,583,118	6,646,231	31 0	28.6	29.8	31.1
Total of all finished products	7,978,955	8,861,060	16,840,015	47.3	47.8	51.2	50.8
Wire nails—kegs of 100 pounds	7,175,418	3,679474	10,854,892	66.1	67.0	70.6	64.8

The aggregate trade of the Steel Corporation has increased considerably since 1901; but in proportion to the business of the whole country it has hardly held its own. We read in one of the recent reports:

Notwithstanding the large sums which have been paid since the organization of the Corporation for increasing the producing capacity by the subsidiary companies, they have only maintained their position in the trade. In 1901 these companies produced 43.2 per cent of the pig iron manufactured in this country, and in 1905, 44.2 per cent. In 1901 these companies produced 66.2 per cent of the Bessemer and open-hearth steel ingots, and in 1905, 60.2 per cent. While these companies do not expect or desire to control the steel industry, they must, so far as proper and practicable, maintain their position, and to do this it has been necessary to expend large sums of money from time to time.[1]

The fact that the proportion of the trade controlled by the company has shown no tendency on the whole to increase, notwithstanding the large outlays made for extensions and improvements, indicates that the Steel Corporation is meeting not a little competition. The fact, too, that a large proportion of the capital of the company has had to forego dividends for more than two years and is now yielding only two per cent shows that no very great control is exercised over the iron and steel industry. As has already been noted, however, the Steel Corporation has during the six years of its history been increasing its holdings of ore lands through which it may in time control the industry by controlling the sources of raw material. This achievement will be difficult; but the best situated and most productive fields are now for the most part held by the corporation. It is principally upon the possession of these lands that the Steel Corporation justifies its huge capitalization. In order to judge the financial stability of the organization it will therefore be necessary to examine its capitalization.

[1] *Fourth Annual Report of U. S. Steel Corporation.*

CHAPTER V

THE CAPITALIZATION OF THE STEEL CORPORATION

§ 1. THE organization of a great consolidation generally takes place in a period of prosperity. It is then that increased earnings and encouraging prospects foster a spirit of enterprise which endeavors to seize the opportunities for increased gains. In a trade like that of iron and steel, characterized by great vicissitudes of demand, the desire to take full advantage of the rising market is peculiarly strong. In order to do this, destructive competition must be prevented; and this necessity gives birth to combinations co-operating to secure the full benefit of the increased demand. It is during a period of rising prices that pools are most easily formed and maintained; and it is during such a time that consolidations are most readily organized. In both cases there is a unity of interest to secure gains which would be much curtailed as a consequence of unlimited competition.

The organization of great corporations or trusts during periods of prosperity has an important effect upon capitalization. In the formation of one of these combinations the capitalization is usually based upon the total earning capacity of the separate plants to be united plus anticipated gains due to good-will, achievement of economies, and real or supposed monopoly advantages. A corporation entering a large combination in a period of flourishing trade is likely to insist upon a higher valuation of its securities than if it entered a consolidation in times of normal business. In not a few cases a strong corporation will remain outside of a

100   [322

combination unless the exchange of securities is based upon its maximum earnings. A corporation, therefore, which is a consolidation of pre-existing corporations or consolidations, is almost inevitably more highly capitalized than normal conditions would justify.

§ 2. The United States Steel Corporation was formed under conditions similar to those which have given birth to consolidations in general. The year 1901 was a year of great prosperity in the iron and steel trade; and the three preceding years, with the exception of a temporary depression during the second half of 1900, constituted a period of increasing demand and rising prices. As has already been indicated, it was the threat of a severe competition in the face of a promising market which was the occasion of the corporation's formation. The corporations which became parts of the new organization at its beginning, though suffering from the depression of 1900, had enjoyed a period of considerable prosperity. In the exchange of securities most of these concerns received a bonus on their previous capitalizations; and thus the total capital of the Steel Corporation was considerably in excess of the combined capitals of its constituent companies.

§ 3. The capital stock of the eight original companies which entered the steel consolidation aggregated $617,070,200. Of this amount $160,000,000 was common stock of the Carnegie Company. In addition to this capital stock was a bonded debt of $191,341,271.72, of which $160,000,000 were Carnegie bonds. In the transfer of securities the Carnegie stocks were paid for in first mortgage bonds in the ratio of $1500 bonds per $1000 stock. The remaining stock of the original eight companies was increased to $719,999,395. The new issues compared with the old are shown by the table on the following page:[1]

[1] From Circular of J. P. Morgan & Co.

CAPITALIZATION OF THE UNITED STATES STEEL CORPORATION

	OLD.		NEW.	
	Preferred.	Common.	Preferred.	Common.
Federal Steel Co..........................	$53,260,900	$40,484,300	$60,446,362	$49,970,623
American Steel & Wire Co	40,000,000	50,000,000	47,000,000	51,250,000
National Tube Co	40,000,000	40,000,000	53,520,000	50,000,000
National Steel Co......................	27,000,000	32,000,000	33,750,000	40,000,000
American Tin Plate Co	18,325,000	28,000,000	28,506,250	35,000,000
American Steel Hoop Co.............	14,000,000	19,000,000	14,000,000	19,000,000
American Sheet Steel Co.............	24,500,000	24,500,000	24,500,000	24,500,000
Carnegie Steel Co......................	....	64,000,000	98,277,120	90,279,040
		(96,000,000 changed to bonded debt of $144,000,000)		
Total stock	$217,085,900	$399,984,300	$359,999,732	$359,999,663
Total stock..............	$617,070,200		$719,999,395	
Increase in total stock.....		$102,929,195		

From this table it will be seen that at the formation of the United States Steel Corporation the stock of the original companies, with the exception of the American Steel Hoop and American Sheet Steel companies, was considerably augmented on the exchange of securities. The difference between the old and new issues of stock was $102,-929,195, to which should be added $144,000,000 of first-mortgage bonds—making a total increase in the capital of the original eight companies of $246,929,195. This represents an increase of capital due to transfer of stock of more than forty per cent.

The capital stock of the American Bridge Company and the Lake Superior Consolidated Iron Mines—both of which entered the Steel Corporation soon after its organization—was likewise increased on the exchange of securities. The old issues of stock outstanding of these two companies was $92,212,049. On the transfer of shares, this stock was increased to $147,705,632, the difference being $55,493,583. Adding this difference to the increase in the stock of the original eight corporations, we see that the capitalization of the United States Steel Corporation was $302,422,778 more than the total capitalization of the ten great companies of which it was first formed.

The aggregate stock capital issued to the ten companies mentioned amounted to $867,705,027. There was issued in addition to this amount $50,000,000 stock—$25,000,000 preferred and $25,000,000 common—in payment for $25,-000,000 cash. The remaining stock of the authorized issue of $1,100,000,000 was left for the pay of the syndicate and as treasury stock for future use. The capital stock issued at the time of the first annual report was $1,018,583,600, of which $508,302,500 was common and $510,281,100 preferred.

§ 4. This capitalization was greater than that of any other

industrial concern in existence and attracted much public attention. The question naturally arises, how far is this huge capitalization justified? Regarding the basis of the capitalization of companies and combinations, two general opinions are held: First, that the amount of capital should be limited by the actual value of the property owned, or should be strictly related to such value; Second, that it should be dependent upon the earning capacity of the company. The second basis of capitalization is the one preferred by most business men. Under competitive conditions, however, these two bases will tend to correspond. It is only under advantages, monopolistic in nature, that the capitalization of earnings is likely to exceed in any considerable degree a capitalization based upon the value of the properties owned.

It has already been noted that the Steel Corporation was organized in a period of prosperity. Just previous to this organization, the eight original constituent companies were paying full dividends on their preferred stock and managed to make payments on the common stock. During the year 1900, the latter half of which was a period of depression, the different interests consolidated made the following profits: [1]

Carnegie Steel Company	$39,000,000
Moore Companies	22,000,000
Federal Steel Company	15,000,000
National Tube Company	13,000,000
American Steel & Wire Company	7,000,000
Total	$96,000,000

A capitalization of a billion dollars on net earnings of $96,-000,000 does not seem excessive. Notwithstanding a temporary depression during the summer and fall months, the

[1] *Iron Age*, Feb. 28, 1901.

year 1900 was on the whole a prosperous year. The early months constituted a period of exceptionally large demand for iron and steel goods; and the high prices of the latter part of 1899 continued. The smaller earnings and lower prices of the latter half of the year, though an important factor in the formation of the Steel Corporation, did not serve to make the gains of 1900 typify a season of depression or even of normal earnings. The net earnings of the Steel Corporation during one of its most prosperous years (1902), which was also one of the most prosperous in the iron and steel trade of the country, were $133,308,-763.72;[1] and at that time the Lake Superior Consolidated Iron Mines and the American Bridge Company had been added to the corporation. When the incomes of these two years are compared, and allowance is made for the earnings of the companies added to the Steel combination since its formation, we readily see that the net income of the eight companies in 1900 typify a year of great prosperity.

§ 5. In so far as the capitalization of the Steel Corporation was based upon earnings, it was so based in a period of good times. What the several constituent companies could earn during normal times, or during an epoch of depression, was a matter of uncertainty. In 1896 and 1897 the Carnegie Steel Company is said to have earned between one-sixth and one-seventh of its net income in 1900;[2] while during the same period the Illinois Steel Company passed all dividends and was reported to be falling behind in meeting current expenses.[3] As these two companies were among the most powerful then existing, they may be said to typify conditions which must be taken into consideration in capitalizing an iron and steel combination. Mr. Car-

[1] *First Annual Report,* 1902.
[2] Moody's *Truth About the Trusts,* p. 200.   [3] *Iron Age.*

negie, when referring to the great vicissitudes in the iron and steel trade, declared that steel is either prince or pauper. It seems clear from what has been said that in the formation of the United States Steel Corporation steel was capitalized while it was a prince, and that its periodical descent to the status of pauper was ignored.

The capitalization of the constituent companies themselves was also much in excess of their tangible assets. The consolidations of the Middle West which became parts of the Steel Corporation were, like that corporation, formed during a period of rising prices and prosperous outlook. The firms entering these combinations exchanged their securities in accordance with the outlook for increased earnings.[1] As in other cases, in the division of stocks into common and preferred, the former came to represent what is vaguely called " good-will " and " future gains due to combination," while the preferred stock alone stood for tangible assets. This division was by no means definitely made in all cases. Nevertheless, the common stock of these corporations represented, in whole or in part, intangible property. In at least one case, good will was included in the preferred stock—the common stock representing only anticipations of future profits and pay of the promoter.

One of the clearest cases of this tendency toward inflated capitalization is that of the American Tin Plate Company. Mr. Reid, the president of that company, testified before the Industrial Commission that $28,000,000 common stock and $18,000,000 preferred stock entered into the capitalization of that corporation; that the $18,000,000 preferred was supposed to represent the cash value of the plants as going concerns, including ordinary good-will, and that all the common represented hope of future success and pay of the

[1] *Report Industrial Commission*, vol. i, pp. 857, 863, 864, 883, 885.

promoter.[1]   He stated further, that as the establishments were bought as going concerns at a time when business was prosperous, and when the vendors felt themselves in a position to make good terms, the prices for which they sold were high, so that all the stock taken together would probably represent from three to five times the cost value of the plants themselves under ordinary conditions.   It was testified by Mr. Graham, one of the vice-presidents of the same company, that in the transfer of securities, when the company was formed, the vendors had the option of receiving $100 cash for each share of stock, or accepting $100 each, in preferred and common stock.   As a result of this option two hundred dollars of stock was preferred to one hundred dollars cash.

The National Tube Company seems to have been capitalized in a manner very similar to that of the Tin Plate Company.   In the capitalization of the National Steel, the American Steel Hoop, and the American Sheet Steel companies [2] the preferred stocks alone represented tangible assets, and the common stock, good will, expectation of future profits, and pay of promoters.   As more than half the stock of these companies was common it will be seen that their capitalization represented very largely intangible assets.

The American Steel and Wire Company was capitalized at $80,000,000.   Mr. Gates, in his testimony before the Industrial Commission, stated that probably $50,000,000 to $60,000,000 might be considered the actual value of the plants.[3]   This estimate, however, was probably too large, as the value placed upon some seventy per cent of the plants in 1897 and 1898 by Mr. Morgan was $28,000,000.   It is

---

[1] *Report of the Industrial Commission,* vol. i, pp. 866, 884.

[2] *Ibid.,* vol. i, pp. 944, 957, 958, 959, 962, 963, 967.

[3] *Ibid.,* vol. i, p. 1021.

more probable that the actual value of the plants of the company was represented by about half the full capitalization.

The Federal Steel Company was in like manner capitalized beyond the value of its plant and property holdings. Before the close of 1899 some $99,000,000 of stock had been issued by this corporation. The book value of all the property of this organization was placed by experts at $45,000,000,[1] although some allowance must be made for an appreciation in the value of its ore and coal properties and for its cash assets.[2] The constituent companies of this corporation with their issues of stock at the time of the formation of the Federal Steel Company were as follows:

Illinois Steel Company	$18,650,000
Minnesota Iron Company	16,500,000
Elgin, Joliet, & Eastern R. R.	6,000,000
Lorain Steel Company (of Ohio)	9,000,000
Lorain Steel Company (of Penn.)	3,000,000
Total	$53,150,000

On this combined capitalization some $53,000,000 of preferred and $46,000,000 of common stock were issued.[3]

§ 6. From what has been said concerning the seven companies mentioned, it will be seen that at the time of their formation practically all the common stock represented such intangible things as good will and expectations of future success. Some $240,000,000 of the stock of these companies thus stood for intangible assets. On entering the United States Steel Corporation, the capitalization of these

---

[1] *Iron Age*, Oct. 26, 1899, p. 35, and *Report of the Industrial Commission*, vol. i, pp. 986, 987.

[2] *Report of the Industrial Commission*, vol. i, pp. 986, 987.

[3] See terms of exchange for each share in *Commercial and Financial Chronicle*, Sept. 10, 1898, p. 530.

consolidations was still further increased over $74,000,000.
If there had been no material improvements and extensions in the plants of these combinations and no increase in
the value of their ore and coal properties, it could be said
that of the $531,000,000 of stock issued to these companies,
more than $300,000,000 represented no visible form of
property.

The Carnegie Steel Corporation and the Lake Superior
Consolidated Iron Mines had no preferred stock. Their
capitalizations were not so disproportionate to the value of
their plants and property holdings. Indeed, considering
the growing value of the ore property in the Lake Superior
region, it may be questioned if the second of these companies was not under-capitalized. The securities of both
these organizations, as has already been noted, were purchased at a heavy premium; and thus was added to an already inflated capitalization an increased issue of stock
which stood for something other than visible assets.

§ 7. Viewed, however, in the light of conditions existing
in the years from 1898 to 1901, this enormous capitalization was the outcome of certain influences which forced
matters to take the turn they did. It has been popularly
pointed out that Mr. Morgan of his own volition brought
the various steel consolidations of the Middle West and
East together in a larger combination, then overloaded
the whole aggregation with half a billion dollars or more
of watered capitalization, then ordered dividends to be paid
on this capitalization, and that as a result of this wild financiering there followed inevitably the crash of 1903 and
1904. The public forgets that this financiering was closely
related to the conditions under which the Steel Corporation
and its constituent companies were organized. After the
depression of the middle nineties there was ushered in a
period of almost unexampled prosperity in the iron and

steel trade. The prosperous outlook gave an impetus to the formation of combinations, and at the same time enabled companies entering these combinations to exact a good price for their securities or properties. This was especially true of the larger and more flourishing of these firms or companies. The capitalization of both the Steel Corporation and the combinations of which it is composed was influenced by the relatively high earning capacity consequent upon an epoch of great demand and high prices.

The conditions in the steel trade situation in the opening months of 1901 which operated to produce an exaggerated capitalization were briefly as follows: The stability of the leading steel interests of the country was threatened by what promised to be a disastrous competition. To prevent this competition and secure the full benefits of the promising outlook for large gains in the immediate future, a union of some sort had to be formed. The device resorted to was that of a holding company.[1] In order that the new consolidation should fulfill its purpose, all the larger corporations must be controlled, and particularly the Carnegie Company. The prosperous times and consequent large profits enabled these interests to exact a good price for their securities. The Carnegie Steel Company, the purchase of whose securities has been a theme of much comment, may serve as an example. In the year 1900 this company's net earnings were $39,000,000.[2] Such earnings enabled Mr. Carnegie to exact a price which he could not have secured a few years before when the profits of the company were only six or seven million dollars. It was absolutely necessary that the Carnegie interests should be controlled. " To control the Carnegie interests meant to purchase them; and to purchase them meant to pay Mr. Andrew Carnegie's

[1] See chapters iii and iv.   [2] *Iron Age*, Feb. 28, 1901.

price for them,"[1] and Mr. Carnegie's price was nearly half a billion dollars.

An era of prosperity in giving a stimulus to the formation of great consolidations therefore acts in a way to promote undue capitalization. In an industry characterized by great variations of trade the earning capacity in such a period is likely to be greatly in excess of the income under normal conditions. It was the high earnings of a prosperous period that were in a sense capitalized in the larger organization of the iron and steel trade. It is thus seen that the vicissitudes of the industry were an important factor in the high capitalization of the Steel Corporation and the consolidations of which it is composed.

§ 8. What has been said concerning the large capitalization of the Steel Corporation and the consolidations of which it is composed refers to the periods of their organization. Since that time there have been material additions to their plants and cash on hand. The value of their ore and coal lands has also very greatly augmented. This increase in property holdings has unquestionably brought the tangible assets of the corporation nearer to its nominal capitalization. How much is to be credited to this increase is a matter of individual judgment. Between the years 1899 and 1901 the values added to the property controlled would, according to officers of the corporation, amount to no less than $175,000,000. This, of course, includes mainly an increase in the value of real property and, to a much less extent, additions to plants and cash on hand. Thus in the case of the Federal Steel Company the book value of the properties of the corporation, estimated at $45,000,000, did not include $10,000,000 cash on hand, nor increases in the value of real property. Some coal land which was

[1] Moody's *Truth About the Trusts,* p. 200.

put in at $500 an acre was later sold for twice that amount, and for a mine costing the company $75,000 as much as $600,000 was subsequently offered.

Since the Steel Corporation was organized there have been large appropriations for the acquisition of new mineral properties and additions to the existing plants. Besides the ordinary expenditures for maintenance of plant, this organization during the first four years and a quarter of its history paid out in such improvements and acquisitions $184,500,000 [1] or between five and six millions more than had been paid out in dividends. Some seventy-five million dollars are to be appropriated for the equipment of the steel plants at Gary, Indiana.

§ 9. What the present value of the properties of the Steel Corporation is, is a question on which considerable divergence of opinion exists. What is held to be its most important asset consists of ore and coal property of rather indeterminate, though great, value. It is this property which is the doubtful factor in ascertaining the extent of the visible assets of the corporation. In Mr. Schwab's opinion the question whether or not the company is over-capitalized depends upon the value that is to be placed upon its unmined ore and coking coal. The value of ore and coal, in his judgment should be considered greater from the fact that the Lake Superior ores and the Connellsville coking coal are apparently limited, and so far as one can judge from the present outlook, iron in this country will be exhausted within a comparatively short time.[2] It should be said, however, that the addition of a large capitalization representing values of unmined ore is not usual, although it may have a certain basis of justification.

[1] *Iron Age*, Oct. 5, 1905, p. 884. See reports of Steel Corporation, 1902-05.

[2] *Report of the Industrial Commission*, vol. 13, pp. 464, 467, 472.

In 1902 when the plan for converting $200,000,000 of preferred stock into bonds was announced, the question of capitalization became one of the determining points in suits brought to prevent the proposed conversion. In one of the suits an affidavit was made to the effect that the plants and properties of the corporation could be duplicated for about $300,000,000 and that the total properties including good will and organization were not worth $500,000,000. Another affidavit stated that the plants of the Carnegie Company, representing 44 per cent of the productive capacity of the Steel Corporation, had been valued on March 12, 1900, by the partners of the Carnegie Company at $75,-000,000. This statement was made in answer to Mr. Frick's bill of complaint, and said it was a " full, fair, and accurate valuation of these assets." The value of all the properties of the corporation was declared to be not more than $200,000,000.

In behalf of the corporation, Mr. Schwab made a detailed statement of the value of its properties. In valuing these assets he employed two leading principles,—the cost of duplication, and the profits derived from their possession. No allowance was made for good-will, patents, trademarks, and the like. The items, grouped under eight general divisions, are as follows:

1. Iron-ore properties	$700,000,000	
2. Plants, mills, fixtures, equipment	300,000,000	
3. Coal and coke fields (87,589 acres)	100,000,000	
4. Transportation properties	80,000,000	after deducting $40,340,000 of bonded debt.
5. Blast furnaces	48,000,000	
6. Natural gas fields	20,000,000	
7. Limestone properties	4,000,000	
8. Cash and cash assets	214,278,000	
Total	$1,466,278,000	

The valuation placed upon the properties in Mr. Schwab's statement exceeded the capitalization by over $100,000,000. Regarding the statements sworn to in connection with the Carnegie-Frick litigation of 1900, that $75,000,000 represented a "full, fair and accurate valuation" of the Carnegie Steel Company's assets, it was shown by Mr. James J Campbell, auditor and assistant secretary of the Carnegie Company, that the properties of that organization had been carried on the books for many years at original costs; and that no allowance had ever been made for money expended for improvements, some of which far exceeded the original outlay. The real property of the company had also with the increased demand for iron and steel goods risen in value.

In the above statement, the figures given for the value of plants, mills, equipment, transportation properties, and blast furnaces are probably conservative. The item of cash and cash assets is, at least, doubtful; and the items of coal and ore properties, are not much more than guesses. It is to be noted that more than half the assets, as given by Mr. Schwab, is ore and coal land,—the ore land alone being figured at $700,000,000. In this latter estimate, Mr. Schwab capitalizes unmined ore, of which he believes there is a rather limited quantity which will at no very remote day be exhausted. In not a few instances, he has insisted upon the importance of this property as the greatest asset of the Steel Corporation.

§ 10. The capitalization of natural mineral resources is a subject on which financiers, captains of industry, and investors hold widely divergent views. It is one thing to mortgage the future and quite another to value property at its present earning capacity. If the possession of a mineral deposit or a group of deposits confers a monopoly, its valuation will be determined by considerations radically different from those governing the appraisal of raw material in the ground whose possessor must compete with the owners of other deposits.   Even where a supposed monopoly exists, the condition may suddenly change by the rise of competition in some distant part of the globe.   It is not very long ago since the Lake Superior mines of copper were deeply affected by the outpouring of great quantities of rich ore from Butte.   The flood of cheap iron ores from the Mesaba range affected not only the Eastern iron workers, but iron producers all over the world.   The risk of new discoveries is one which established owners of mineral property always run; and this risk should be reckoned with. Furthermore, the acquisition of a monopoly in the case of iron ore is rather remote, and out of the question in the case of coal.   The control of the most favorably located deposits from an economic point of view is another matter. It may be figured that the ownership of Lake Superior iron ore mines is equivalent to so much a ton on steel under the cost of producers drawing their supply of raw material from other sources.   Even such figuring has its element of danger.   Technical progress may render natural advantages less important.   The monopoly of Bessemer ore, for example, was deeply affected by the introduction of the basic process.

Risks like these should find an expression in some discount of the capitalization of mineral deposits.   A cardinal question, however, is whether or not it is wise to capitalize future earnings at all, assuming that they are secure.   Capital implies interest or dividend obligations; and charges on a future output of metal may necessitate a forced utilization to meet such obligations.   This may become a serious menace to the industry itself and the collateral branches of manufacture depending upon it.   It has been computed, too, that it would require about five dollars per ton of steel output to pay interest on the Steel Corporation's nominal capitalization at the rate of seven per cent, whereas other competitive concerns can get off with about a dollar and a half per ton of steel produced [1]—the latter's capacity of output in relation to nominal capital being much greater. If the Steel ˉCorporation has stores of raw material relatively greater and better than others, this fact justifies a larger capitalization per unit of manufactured product. The capitalization, however, should not be disproportionate to this differential advantage.

Nevertheless, it must be said that ore properties all over the world are rapidly growing in value. The ore question is assuming a dominant place; and the high estimate placed by Mr. Schwab upon the value of the holdings of the Steel Corporation in the Lake Superior region will probably appear modest within a very few years. The importance attached to rich deposits of ore is indicated not only by the action of domestic producers securing their sources of raw material, even at considerable expense, but by the action of foreign governments in their attempts to conserve the home supply. It is only last year that Germany, after some anxiety over a proposal by Spain to impose a tax on exports of Spanish ore to Germany, concluded an arrangement by which the threat was withdrawn in return for some reciprocal benefits. The governments of both Norway and Sweden have proposed steps for the limitation of iron ore exports; and it is very possible that the latter government will take under its control the north Swedish ore properties. Owing to the increasing difficulty in obtaining Scandinavian ores, prominent Rhenish Westphalian producers of iron and steel have asked the German Ministry of Public Works for special rates for transport of ore from

---

[1] *Report of the British Iron Trade Commission on American Conditions,* by J. S. Jeans, p. 191.

the French district of Briey.[1]   These measures are all indicative of a fear of future scarcity of iron ore; and this
fear is giving rise to serious concern in political as well as
industrial circles.

Upon the world's apparently limited supply of ore the
demand for steel is pressing with increasing urgency.   Going back twenty-five years we find that the steel rail was not
only the back-bone of the steel industry but its body and
bulk.   In 1881 production of steel rails in the United States
was 1,210,285 gross tons, while in the same year the Bessemer steel ingot production amounted to 1,374,247 gross
tons, or only 163,962 tons more, and the output of open
hearth ingots was 131,202 tons.   To-day, not only is the
steel rail production nearly three times that of 1881, but
even this production is only a fraction of the entire steel
trade.   The increased use of wire nails and barb wire is
making the manufacture of wire rods nearly as important
as that of steel rails.   The production of structural shapes
amounted to 360,005 tons in 1894.   In 1902 it had increased to 1,300,326 tons.   The tonnage of vessels built of
steel in the ten years beginning with 1880 averaged 35,000
tons of new capacity a year.   In the next ten years the average was 86,000 tons a year.   In the five years beginning
with 1900 the average was 248,000 tons a year.   The use
of the steel car is adding some eight or nine hundred thous-
and tons to the steel consumption of the country.   The importance of the steel tie as a feeder to the industry, once its
use is established, can hardly be overestimated.   The production and consumption of iron and steel are increasing
faster than population.   In terms of pig iron, the per capita
increase of production in this country may be shown as
follows:

[1] *Iron Age*, Mar. 7, 1907, p. 75.

1880.............................. 171 pounds.
1890.............................. 329   "
1900.............................. 399   "
1905.............................. 619   "
1906.............................. 662   "   (estimated).

Barring the possibility of the discovery of very extensive and cheaply worked ore fields in other regions, the ever-widening stream of iron and steel consumption will add greatly to the value of the holdings of the Steel Corporation in the Lake Superior region.   Even the high price to be paid for the Great Northern properties recently transferred to the corporation is probably small in proportion to the future value of those properties.   Nevertheless the contingency of radical changes in the industry due to new discoveries or invention remains.   While time may justify the sagacity of the men who attached a high value to the sources of ore supply, there nevertheless remains a considerable element of danger in the capitalization of a future asset.

§ 11. That the United States Steel Corporation has been enabled to face not a little competition, and during a year at least of considerable depression to meet its interest obligations on some $500,000,000 of bonded indebtedness and to pay in addition seven per cent dividends on $360,000,000 of preferred stock argues in favor of the high value of its plants and properties.   We may dismiss without comment the contention of one of the witnesses in the Hodge suit brought to test the legality of the bond conversion that the tangible assets of the company should not be valued at more than $200,000,000.   The earning capacity of the corporation during the six years of its existence is at least some index to the value of its assets.   If the amount paid out in interest on bonds and in dividends on stock during 1904, the most trying year of its existence, is capitalized at five per cent the capitalization would amount in round numbers to $974,759,000. The dividends of the Standard Oil Company in 1905 capitalized in the same way would amount to nearly $800,000,000.[1] A conservative estimate of the value of Standard Oil property, exclusive of monopoly advantages places it at about $300,000,000. The Steel Corporation is not the monopoly that the Standard Oil Company is, and yet its dividends and interest payments during the darkest year of its history capitalized at five per cent amounts to $974,759,000.

It must be said, however, that during more than two years no dividends were paid on $508,300,000 of common stock, and only two per cent is being paid at the present time. How much of this stock represents tangible property is difficult to determine. From what has been said concerning the consolidations which became parts of the Steel Corporation, the common stock must be looked upon as representing in large measure good will and future gains. It is essentially capitalization of future returns. It should be remembered, however, that the Steel Corporation, as was shown in the preceding chapter, has been steadily adding to its previous holdings of ore and coal lands. As the demand for iron and steel has greatly increased in recent years and gives promise of further increase in the future, these lands are likely to be a very considerable addition to the assets of the company.

The market value of the outstanding securities of the Steel Corporation, if taken through a long series of years, would tend to give a fairly accurate measure of the value of its properties. But the corporation has been in existence only six years; and more than two-thirds of that period has been exceptionally prosperous. Although it ex-

[1] *Commercial and Financial Chronicle.*

perienced an epoch of depression in the latter part of 1903 and during the year 1904, it has not yet been compelled to withstand hard times comparable to those of the middle nineties. Nevertheless, it is of some interest to compare the par and market values of the corporation's securities.

The par value of the securities of the United States Steel Corporation at the close of the year, 1906, was in round numbers $1,340,000,000. In the first year of its existence, it was slightly less. In April, 1901, the approximate market value of all the outstanding securities was $1,265,-000,000. By December, 1903, this value had shrunk to about $760,000,000.[1] During the closing months of 1904 there was some revival in the iron and steel trade with a consequent rise in value of the corporation's securities. During 1905 and 1906 the earnings steadily increased, and the latter of these years showed the largest net income of any year in the corporation's history. This period of prosperity has continued to the present time. As a consequence of this prosperity the stocks and bonds of the company have been quoted at high figures. During the month of February, 1907, the market value of the outstanding securities of the Steel Corporation approximated $1,170,000,000.[2] The quotations of these securities, it must be remembered, represent their value during a period of " good times."

§ 12. The future stability of the Steel Corporation will depend not a little upon the character of this huge capitalization. Reference has already been made to the conversion of preferred stock into bonds. In the spring of 1902, when the conversion of preferred stock into bonds was first proposed, the bonded debt of the corporation and its constitu-

---

[1] Based upon quotations in the *Commercial and Financial Chronicle.* See also Moody's *Truth about the Trusts*, p. 201.

[2] Based upon stock and bond quotations in New York *Sun.*

ent companies was, in round numbers, $350,000,000. As indicated in a previous chapter,[1] the plan was to exchange $200,000,000 of preferred stock for a like amount of five per cent second mortgage bonds, and to issue $50,000,000 additional bonds for the same amount of cash. The ostensible motive which prompted this proposal was the need of money for additions and improvements in the plants of the corporation. It was further urged that such a conversion would result in an annual saving of a million and a half dollars. In view of the large surplus remaining to the company after paying all charges and dividends at the end of the first year, the need of saddling the corporation with such an increase in its debt has seemed questionable to many. The argument, too, that by the conversion, $1,500,000 a year would be saved has seemed almost ludicrous to some for an organization whose net income for the same year was over $133,000,000.

It was contended by the executive committee, however, that the expenditure of about $25,000,000 for improvements would add from $10,000,000 to $15,000,000 to the yearly profits. The committee further stated: " That these expenditures could be met gradually from surplus earnings the management does not doubt; but this would necessitate extending them over a period of years, and correspondingly would postpone the realization of the profits which, by the immediate use of money, could be obtained promptly." [2]

The proposal as originally announced was never fully carried into effect. Of the proposed $200,000,000, only $150,000,000 of the preferred stock was exchanged for bonds. The bonded debt, however, of the corporation and its subsidiary companies was increased to over $500,000,-

[1] *Cf.* ch. iv.
[2] Circular to Stockholders, Apr. 17, 1902, p. 2.

ooo, and has thus become considerably more than one-third of the total capitalization.

Whether or not the financial stability of the corporation has been affected by the bond conversion depends partly upon the value of the company's properties and partly upon the steadiness of its income. That the assets of the corporation are great and that all indications point to an increase in the value of its ore properties, we have already seen. When it is remembered, however, that the iron and steel trade is peculiarly subject to fluctuations, this exchange of securities must seem a rather doubtful expedient of corporate financiering. That the management of the organization is confident of its ability to secure a large volume of trade, even in dull times, is shown in the contract transferring the Hill holdings which pledges the corporation to a minimum output of 8,250,000 tons of ore from these properties in 1917 at a royalty of $16,417,500. This royalty must be paid, if the properties are retained, irrespective of trade conditions. Here, however, the corporation is safeguarded in a measure by the reservation to itself of the option of terminating the lease on January 1, 1915.[1] In the case of the bonded indebtedness incurred by the conversion of preferred stock the corporation is to some extent protected by the provision which allows a lapse of two years after failure to pay interest, before foreclosure proceedings can be commenced. This provision, however, while by no means an unimportant safeguard, would hardly preserve the integrity of the corporation in a period of prolonged depression, like the middle nineties. While the Steel Corporation may be said to have had a steadying effect upon the industry, the vicissitudes of the trade are nevertheless so great that a liberal margin should be al-

[1] See *Fifth Annual Report*.

lowed between normal earnings on the one hand and fixed charges and operating expenses on the other.

As is well known it is a fixed policy of good railroad financiering that earnings should never fall below fixed charges and operating expenses. As far as possible, it has been the policy of successful railroads to reduce fixed charges and replace bonds by preferred stock. The Chicago, Milwaukee and Saint Paul Railroad, for example, has upwards of $40,000,000 of seven per cent preferred shares. The conversion of this respectable sum of capital into five per cent bonds would save that company $800,000 annually and enable it to pay nearly two per cent extra on its common stock. Instead of embarking upon such a policy, the company made some old mortgages convertible into stock, and has converted $30,000,000 of its funded debt during the last twenty or thirty years. The opposite policy on the part of the Steel Corporation, engaged in a business far more specialized and more exposed to changes in trade conditions than railroad traffic has excited much attention and not a little criticism. It is a business principle that it is never wise to substitute fixed charges which must be met for dividend payments which can be postponed. Such an axiom, it would seem, even so powerful a corporation cannot afford to disregard.

Whether or not the bond conversion has seriously endangered the future integrity of the Steel Corporation is a question which is difficult to answer. In 1903 Mr. James H. Bridge said that the revenues of the corporation could be reduced by one-third without necessitating a reduction in the present rate of dividend on preferred stock.[1] It should be noted, however, that Mr. Bridge spoke in view of the prosperous conditions existing in the year 1902 and

[1] *Commercial and Financial Chronicle*, 1903, pp. 2039-2109.

the early part of 1903. The net earnings for 1902 were $133,308,000, and for 1903, $109,177,000. In the year 1904, these earnings had declined to $73,176,000, making a decrease of over $60,000,000 from the net income of 1902. When it is remembered that the annual dividends on the preferred stock amount to only $25,219,677, and that in the year 1904, after the payment of this dividend, the interest on the bonded indebtedness and the various charges for depreciation, replacement, and sinking funds, only $5,047,800 remained as a surplus, it can be seen how near to the danger limit a year of severe depression may bring the corporation.

§ 13. In summary of this chapter it may be said that the tendency toward consolidation is most marked in times of prosperity. Such periods are periods of more than normal earnings, and this is especially the case with the iron and steel industry. The capitalization of a combination formed in such a period is largely based upon the extraordinary earnings of the time, and thus tends to be in excess of the tangible assets of the organization. The Steel Corporation and the consolidations of which it is composed were formed in years of exceptional prosperity and were thus largely overcapitalized. In a rough way it may be said that the preferred stock represented the value of plants and properties; and the common stock stood for supposed future values. The capitalization of the Steel Corporation was much in excess of the total for all its constituent companies, most of which were already over-capitalized. All these organizations expended large sums in the improvement and extension of their plants and thus added to their real capital. This capital was still further increased by the growing demand for iron and steel goods, which gave additional value to ore and coal properties. These properties are now considered the most valuable asset of the Steel Corporation, and in Mr. Schwab's estimate are worth $800,000,000. This imputed value, however, is based upon a supposed scarcity of ore and coal in the not-far-off future. The possibility of the discovery of new ore fields, as well as changes in the technical requirements of the iron and steel industry renders such imputed valuation rather uncertain. The increasing use of steel for building purposes, etc., makes it probable, however, that these lands will continue to be a great asset to the corporation. It is difficult to determine the value of the plants and properties of the Steel Corporation; but it is undoubtedly greater than many of the estimates made by those contesting the validity of the bond conversion. While the value of the properties of the company is unquestionably high and its resources great, its bonded debt, increased by the conversion of $150,000,000 of preferred stock, is a possible menace to its future financial integrity.

CHAPTER VI

The Steel Corporation and Prices

§ 1. The most important, economically speaking, as well as the most interesting question concerning a consolidation or trust is its influence on prices. The nature of this influence depends in large measure on the control which the organization exercises over the industry in which it is engaged. Like the pool, the consolidation owes its origin to attempts to restrict competition; and its success in this endeavor is indicated by its influence on market conditions. Whether or not a business organization exercises such a control, and what is the extent of this control, assuming it to exist, are questions difficult to answer and involving a multitude of considerations. Changes in the demand for goods, variations in technical processes, vicissitudes in labor cost, the limitation or opening up of sources of raw material, and legislation limiting the field of competition by imposition of tariff duties, are all factors in increasing or diminishing prices independent of any direct influence from monopolistic control.

In the attempt, moreover, to estimate this influence, price quotations, which furnish the most important data, must be accepted with considerable reserve. Real and quoted prices are not invariably the same, nor in all cases are the prices to large and small customers. Quoted prices, often inexact, have been notoriously so on a declining market; and at all times the temptation to favor the large customer has been great. In a period, too, of rising demand not only

126   [348

will the quoted prices be paid, but also premiums for prompt delivery. These considerations make any attempt to gauge the influence of a large combination on market conditions rather hazardous. This is especially so when the object is to determine how far a consolidation has been influential in raising or lowering prices. In any very exact estimate of this influence, allowance for these discounts and premiums should be made; and yet it is difficult to measure even approximately these variations from quoted values. In the iron and steel industry this difficulty is enhanced by the fact that discounts and premiums seem to have been more frequent before than since the formation of the Steel Corporation.

§ 2. It may be said, however, that price quotations taken through a series of years do indicate with some approach to accuracy real variations. In so far as they are given for purposes of trade they do, in general, tell what the ordinary consumer has to pay for his goods. In the iron and steel trade they give an adequate idea of the fluctuations to which prices are subject. Notwithstanding numerous deviations from quoted schedules in a declining market, there is a strong disposition to adhere to quoted figures in times of rising prices, and to give fairly accurate quotations in periods of long and extreme depression. They form, therefore, a fairly reliable index of the fluctuations characteristic of the trade.

In order to form some estimate of the influence of the Steel Corporation on prices, it will be necessary to give some attention to iron and steel prices in general. During the last thirty years, in which the industry in the United States has grown to its present predominant position in the markets of the world, the prices of iron and steel have greatly declined. From 1870 to 1900 this decline on the average, according to the Twelfth Census, was considerably more than fifty per cent.[1]   The course of prices is well typified by those of steel rails, which until recently formed the bulk of the country's steel trade.   The price per ton of this commodity averaged $92.91 in 1870; $67.50 in 1880; $31.75 in 1890; and $32.29 in 1900.[2]   Late in 1900 the price sank to $26.00.   During the depression of the middle nineties prices were lower than ever before or since—steel rails selling as low as $17.00 per ton in June, 1898.[3]   Since April, 1901, steel rails have been quoted at $28.00.

As has already been noted, the prices of iron and steel goods are subject to great fluctuations; and quotations for single years may lead to mistaken conclusions.   It may be said, however, that the three decennial years chosen to illustrate price changes were all years of prosperity; and 1900 was especially so, notwithstanding the mild depression of the fall months.   During thirty years, therefore, prices can be said to have undergone a remarkable reduction.   The consumer in the first decade of the twentieth century gives less than half the price paid by the buyer of 1869 and 1870 for most of his iron and steel.

§ 3.   This price reduction was due in part to the opening up of new sources of raw material, and in part to improvements in technical processes.   In 1870 the country relied for most of its ore on Pennsylvania and other eastern states.   It is true that during the ten preceding years upwards of 3,000,000 tons of iron ore had been shipped from the Lake Superior region; but this amount formed a small percentage of the total product of the country.   The eastern ore while more expensive to mine and more limited in quantity had the advantage of being located near the coal region of the country and within easy distance of the principal markets.

[1] *Twelfth United States Census*, vol. x, p. 8.
[2] *Report of the Industrial Commission*, vol. xiii, p. 625.
[3] *Iron Age*, June 30, 1898.

The change from the use of eastern to Lake Superior ore is associated with the introduction of the Bessemer process.   As was indicated in a previous chapter,[1] the Lake Superior material is largely suited to this process.   During the eighth and ninth decades of the last century the demand for steel in the place of iron for railroads, bridge construction, etc., was growing; and this demand had to be satisfied. Steel had been manufactured east of the Alleghanies largely out of imported pig iron, but at an expense too great for general use.   With the introduction of coke as a fuel and the cheapening of rates for transportation of ores over the Great Lakes, the cost of manufacture was much reduced for the producers west of the Alleghanies, who were in close proximity to the coking-coal areas of the country. The decline in freight rates to eastern markets still further enabled these producers to undersell their competitors east of the Alleghanies.[2]   While all these influences conspired to lower prices, not a little of this reduction is to be attributed to the presence of competition from the new ore region, leading to the final displacement of the eastern product by the more cheaply mined ores of Lake Superior.   Taking the country as a whole, the average cost per ton of iron ore at blast furnaces was approximately $4.60 in 1880, $3.70 in 1890, and less than $3.00 in 1900.

Contemporaneous with the opening up of new ore regions was the development of new processes of manufacture.   Allusion has just been made to the cheapening of costs by the use of coke.   The installation at modern plants of the latest labor-saving machinery and the employment of

[1] *Cf. supra*, ch. ii.

[2] For an excellent account of the effect of the declining freight rate and the protective tariff upon the steel industry of eastern Pennsylvania, see Levy, *Die Stahlindustrie der Vereinigten Staaten von Amerika*, chap. ii.

skilled managers and workmen have also helped to lower prices. This cheapening of manufactures may be illustrated in the case of pig iron. Between the years 1890 and 1899 the average daily product of pig iron at a typical blast furnace plant in Pennsylvania had increased 63.3 per cent. The yield of iron per ton of ore diminished about three per cent. The amount of fuel needed to manufacture a ton of iron declined three per cent; and the requirement of limestone, 25.5 per cent. The cost of ore per ton of iron diminished some 25 per cent; labor cost, 38.9 per cent, and office and incidental expenses, 29.4 per cent. The total cost per ton of iron declined 34.2 per cent.[1] When it is remembered that the costs and conditions of producing pig iron are important factors of price determination in the iron industry, the significance of such an instance, which is fairly typical of the country, can readily be understood.

In steel manufacture there has been a similar cheapening of costs. According to the records of the United States Census, the average cost of materials per ton of finished product was $37.00 in 1880 and $26.00 in 1890. The average output per employee in the same years were respectively 37 and 60 tons; and the average wages per ton of product were $12.10 and $9.40. These figures show that the steel industry made considerable progress during the decade ending with 1890. Great strides were also made in the closing decade of the century. Mr. Kirchhoff, in an address to the American Institute of Mining Engineers, in February, 1899, stated that the cost of producing Bessemer steel ingots had diminished by about one-half between 1887 and 1898. The total cost of producing Bessemer steel ingots declined in the proportion of 100 to 64.39 between the years 1891 and 1898.

[1] *Report of the British Iron Trade Commission*, p. 116.

§ 4. Enough has been said to indicate a great cheapening in the cost of iron and steel goods resulting from the use of cheaper ores and improved technical processes. It would not be correct, however, to attribute all this change to invention and discovery. Cost varies to a considerable extent with the oscillations of trade. A period of depression, for example, is a period of low money wages. The low costs of the middle nineties were due in part to the relatively low wages incident to the hard times of that period. Labor cost, while playing a smaller part in the determination of price in an industry like that of iron and steel than in a trade where little or no machinery is used, is nevertheless a material element.

How far this price tendency was affected by the growth of consolidations in the closing years of the nineteenth century and by the organization of the Steel Corporation at the opening of the twentieth is difficult to estimate with any degree of accuracy. These organizations were formed in a period of extraordinary prosperity. There was a great demand not only for old standard products, but also for material to be put to new uses. New forms of structural material, steel cars, new varieties of wire goods, and the like came into vogue. Demand for all these commodities tended to raise prices far above the level of the middle nineties notwithstanding the low cost of production. In any estimate of the influence of combinations, therefore, allowance must be made for the prosperity of the period.

That the consolidations of the time were a factor influencing prices can be seen in the cases of the American Tin Plate and the American Steel and Wire companies. These companies had something of a monopoly of the market in their respective lines; and this monopoly was reflected in the prices of the period. Shortly after the organization of the American Tin Plate Company in December, 1898, the price of coke tin plate (14x20) was raised from $2.70 per hundred pound box to $3.00 at mill. Quotations in the leading centers of trade in the northeastern part of the country were upwards of $3.20 per hundred pound box. During February, 1899, the average price was $3.55. By the end of the year it was $4.84, and it remained at this figure during a large part of the following year.[1] In like manner after the organization of the American Steel and Wire Company there was a great rise in prices. Wire rods which sold for $20.00 to $22.50 per ton in 1898 were quoted at steadily increasing prices during 1899. By January, 1900, the price had reached $50.00 per ton. Wire nails, which had been quoted at $1.40 to $1.50 per 100-pound keg in 1898, were steadily raised in price during 1899 until they were quoted at $3.20 in the early months of 1900 [2]—a higher figure than that reached under the régime of the notorious wire-nail association of 1895 and 1896.

It is true that the period under consideration was one of increasing demand for iron and steel goods and that rising prices were general. The rise, however, in each case was most marked immediately after the organization of the manufacturing consolidation. The difference, too, between English and American prices was increased notwithstanding the fact that the English as well as the American industry was enjoying a period of great prosperity and rising prices. In the case of coke tin plate the price per hundred pound box at New York City during the last seven months of 1898 ranged from twenty to thirty-five cents above that of the English product—excluding tariff duty—at the same place. While prices in both England and the United States

---

[1] *Iron Age*, 1898-99, *op. cit., passim.*

[2] *Report of the Industrial Commission*, vol. xiii, p. 558.

were rising, immediately after the formation of the American Tin Plate Company the difference between the figures for the two countries became very pronounced. At the organization of the trust this difference was increased to sixty cents, and two months later to $1.30. From the time the Tin Plate Company was organized to the time the Steel Corporation was formed, the difference in price per hundred pound box between English and American coke tin plate was more than one dollar. While the conditions of the time favored high prices, these figures indicate that consolidation influenced the situation very appreciably.

Previous to this era of consolidation prices had been influenced by pooling combinations; but this influence was not so general. One of the most extraordinary cases of price manipulation in any industry was that of the wire nail association alluded to above. In the spring of 1895 a wire nail pool or association raised the price of wire nails from $1.45 a keg to $1.80. A month later the price was raised to $2.15. In another month it rose to $2.65, then to $2.85, where it remained to the end of February, 1896. Another rise brought the price up to $3.00, where it stayed for two months. From the first of May to the end of October the quoted price of wire nails per keg was $3.15. During all this period the producers of cut nails co-operated with the association in raising the prices of cut nails in the same proportion as those of wire nails, so that the consumer was unable to save himself from this extortion by substituting one commodity for the other. In November the pool broke and the price soon fell to $1.50. Just before the pool was formed the difference in price between wire nails and No. 11 wire, out of which the nails are made, was about twenty-five cents per one hundred pounds. After the pool was organized this difference increased to $1.90, although the price of No. 11 wire varied but little during the whole period.

The wire nail association was one of the most flagrant instances of price manipulation in the history of combinations.   It was especially so in view of the low cost of the material out of which wire nails are manufactured.   Concerning this pool the *Iron Age* says:

The managers of the Nail Association can take to themselves the credit of having developed a stronger sentiment against combinations than any other single agency.   They have aroused an intensely bitter feeling among all classes and conditions of people, which could only have been awakened by making exorbitant prices on an article of such universal consumption as nails.[1]

From what has been said concerning the course of prices in general it is seen that improved processes of manufacture and the opening-up of new sources of raw material have reduced the cost of iron and steel to the consumer. This general trend in the direction of lower prices has at times been interfered with by the formation of pools and combinations—especially during the later nineties.   As has already been indicated, some of the consolidations formed during the period from 1898 to 1900 virtually controlled for a time the output of their special commodities.   When the United States Steel Corporation was organized, embracing as it did these combinations, the new organization seemed like a consolidation of monopolies.   The force of competition which had given consumers the benefit of new inventions and discoveries seemed, for the time at least, completely destroyed.   The London *Engineer* voiced a feeling very widespread on both sides of the Atlantic when it said:

Mr. Morgan and his immediate partners can fix the price of iron and steel.   They are for the moment, at all events, be-

[1] *Iron Age*, Dec. 3d, 1896, p. 1086.

yond the sphere of competition. They can have no competitors in their own country. The American consumer is absolutely in the hands of the trust. They can have no European competitor because the tariff defends them.

In attempting to gauge the influence of the Steel Corporation on prices, it may be well to form some estimate of the validity of this gloomy prediction. As was noted in a previous chapter, the corporation was organized to avoid a threatened competition between concerns engaged largely in different lines of manufacture and to a considerable extent mutually dependent upon one another. These companies were at least quasi-monopolies at the time of their organization. Some of these concerns, like the American Steel and Wire Company, the American Tin Plate Company, and the American Bridge Company, were estimated to control about ninety per cent of the country's output of their principal commodities at the time of their formation. However, during the prosperous period of 1899 and 1900 competing establishments were being organized, and some of these were of formidable proportions. Except where patents had been secured, these independent plants, by the opening of 1901, were making their influence felt in the industrial field. The Steel Corporation did not, therefore, result in a combination of monopolies.

Nor did the Steel Corporation achieve monopoly by securing control over the country's output of iron ore. As was indicated in a previous chapter, its present holdings in the Lake Superior district, although several large additions had been made since its formation, are still in all probability not greatly in excess of two-thirds of the visible supply. As there are large deposits in other parts of the country, complete control over the ore supply is far from having been secured.

§ 5. The fear that the formation of the Steel Corporation would result in a general marking-up of prices due to monopoly control proved unfounded. Prices in general were rising in the early months of 1901; but no very marked advances seem to have taken place as a result of the organization of the new consolidation. A consideration of the general trend of prices immediately before and after the formation of the Steel Corporation will show this.

Bessemer pig iron, which sold for $24.90 per ton in the latter part of 1899 and the early months of 1900, dropped to $13.00 per ton in October of the latter year. It then gradually rose again to $15.50 in March, 1901. In November, 1899, steel billets were quoted at $39.50 per ton, from which abnormal figure they gradually declined to $16.50 in October, 1900, rising again to $21.50 in March, 1901. The price of steel rails, which had risen to $35.00 per ton in 1899 and remained at or near that figure during the first seven months of 1900, fell to $26.00 in November, where it stayed until after the organization of the Steel Corporation. Wire rods which had reached the high figure of $50.00 per ton in January, 1900, were selling at $30.00 in July, and at $33.00 to $35.00 in the opening months of 1901.

The low prices of the latter half of 1900 were due to a mild depression which had set in just previous to the presidential election of that year. The opening months of 1901 were characterized by a revival in trade and rising prices. It was in this period of rising prices that the Steel Corporation was organized. Soon after its formation the price of Bessemer pig iron advanced to $16.75 per ton; that of steel billets to $24.00; that of steel rails to $28.00; and that of wire rods to $38.00. With the exception of steel rails, the prices of none of these commodities remained permanent through the year. Bessemer pig iron declined

to $15.75 per ton and rose agair. to $16.50.   Steel billets
dropped to $23.50 per ton and then rose to $27.00.   Wire
rods were quoted at $39.00 in May and June, but declined
to $34.25 in December.   In these quotations it is worthy
of note that the most conspicuous advance in price was that
of steel billets, of which the Steel Corporation sells but
little; and that there was an appreciable advance in pig
iron which was not sold by the corporation at all.   The
year 1901 was a year of great prosperity, and the advance
in prices was a natural outcome of the increased demand
for goods.   In no case were the quotations marked higher
for the commodities which the Steel Corporation sold in
large quantities than for those which it did not sell at all
or only in small quantities.

The year 1902 was one of the most prosperous in the
history of the iron and steel trade.   Until 1906 it was the
banner year of the Steel Corporation.   Notwithstanding its
great prosperity, prices by no means reached the high level
they had attained in 1899 and 1900.   The brisk trade of
1902 was followed by the depression of 1903 and 1904.
During these years prices declined to relatively low levels,
though not so low as during the middle nineties.   Near
the end of 1904 there was a revival in the iron and steel
trade, followed by the prosperous years 1905 and 1906.
Prices rose to higher figures than at any time since 1902,
and those of crude materials to figures higher than any
since the Steel Corporation was organized.   Quotations
taken from the *Iron Age*, showing the highest and lowest
prices of standard materials in the six years preceding and
the six years succeeding the formation of the Steel Corporation, are given in the following table:

TABLE OF PRICES

	Before the formation of the Steel Corporation.	After the formation of the Steel Corporation.
Foundry pig iron, No. 2, Philadelphia:		
Highest per gross ton	$23.25, Nov. and Dec., 1899.	$26.50, Jan. and Feb., 1907.
Lowest per gross ton	10.25, June, 1897.	14.75, Aug. and Sept., 1901.
Bessemer pig iron, Pittsburg:		
Highest per gross ton	24.90, Dec., 1899, and Jan., 1900.	23.85, Dec., 1906.
Lowest per gross ton	9.25, July, 1897.	12.40, July, 1904.
Steel billets, Pittsburg:		
Highest per gross ton	39.50, Nov., 1899.	32.50, June, 1902.
Lowest per gross ton	13.82, May, 1897.	19.50, Oct., 1904.
Steel rails, Eastern mill:		
Highest per gross ton	35.00, Nov. and Dec., 1899, and March to Aug., 1900.	} 28.00.
Lowest per gross ton	16.50, Nov., 1898.	
Wire rods, Pittsburg:		
Highest per gross ton	50.00, Jan., 1900.	39.00, May–June, 1901.
Lowest per gross ton	20.00, June, 1898.	26.00, Sept., 1904.
Bar iron, Philadelphia and Pittsburg:		
Highest per 100 pounds.........	2.25, Sept., 1800.	1.80, June, 1902.
Lowest per 100 pounds.........	1.00, July, 1898.	1.35, Dec., 1903–Jan., 1904.
Steel tankplate, Pittsburg:		
Highest per 100 pounds.........	3.00, Oct, 1899.	1.85, Nov., 1902.
Lowest per 100 pounds.........	1.00, Aug., 1897, March, 1898.	1.40, Oct.–Nov., 1904.
Steel beams, Philadelphia:		
Highest per 100 pounds.........	2.40 Sept, 1899, to May, 1900.	2.27, July, 1902.
Lowest per 100 pounds.........	1.15, July to Sept., 1897.	1.54, Oct.–Nov., 1904.
Wire nails, Pittsburg:		
Highest per 100 pounds.........	3.20, Jan.–March. 1900.	2.30, March–Sept., 1901.
Lowest per 100 pounds.........	1.25, July and Aug., 1897.	1.60, Sept.–Oct., 1904.

From the preceding table it will be seen that the highest prices quoted in the period succeeding the organization of the Steel Corporation did not reach the high level of 1899 and 1900, except in the case of foundry pig iron, which the corporation does not sell.   Nor are the lowest quotations as low as those of 1897 and 1898.   The Steel Corporation has followed what business men would call a conservative policy.   This policy has doubtless been due to a recognition that control of the productive forces of the industry has not been achieved, and that any attempt to raise prices much above what market conditions will justify would increase the number of competitors already in the field.

The Steel Corporation, however, does produce a large percentage of the wire goods of the country.   Almost seventy per cent of the wire rods are manufactured by this organization, and from sixty-five to seventy per cent of the wire nails.   The prices of these commodities do not seem to have been greatly influenced in any way detrimental to the interests of the consumer.   Immediately after the organization of the Steel Corporation wire rods were raised in price to $38.00 per ton and then to $39.00, after which they gradually declined to $34.25 in December, 1901.   During the year 1899 the average price of wire rods according to the quotations in the *Iron Age* was $36.50 per ton.   During the prosperous year 1902 the price averaged $35.80.   During the same years the average prices of wire nails were respectively $2.45 and $2.00.   Other wire products show similar differences in price which are more favorable to the period succeeding the formation of the Steel Corporation than to the one preceding it.   As in the case of iron and steel products in general a conservative policy has been followed.

The wisdom of this moderate policy may be illustrated

by the case of steel plate.   In February, 1899, the price of
steel plate at Pittsburg was $1.30 per one hundred pounds.
In view of the growing demand for this commodity the
steel-plate pool raised the price to $3.00 in August of that
year.   This price attracted several competitors.   With the
lessened demand of 1900 the rolling mills fought to secure
business; and in July, 1900, the ruinous price of $1.05 was
reached.   Several mills were compelled to go out of business.   With the revival of trade in 1901 and 1902 there
was another great demand for steel plate, due largely to
the steel-car and steel-ship industries.   This price was
raised by the Steel Corporation to $1.60, and maintained
at or near that figure in face of a greatly increasing demand.   New rivals were thus kept out of the industry.
Throughout most of the depression of the latter half of
1903 and 1904 this price continued in force.   The maintenance of a profitable price during a period of slackened
trade was thus made easier by the policy of a reasonable
price in good times.

§ 6.   In line with this general policy is the attitude of the
Steel Corporation toward the prices of raw materials.   The
Steel Corporation is engaged primarily in the manufacture
and sale of rolled or finished products.   Owning, however, a
large percentage of the best ore fields in the country, its
influence on the price of ore is important.   In 1901 it fixed
the price of iron ore at $1.25 less per ton than was paid
during the season of 1900.   The reason for this action is
not clear.   Mr. Schwab vaguely intimated that this act
showed that there was no attempt at securing excessively
high prices.[1]   It may be said in this connection that the
Steel Corporation at this time purchased much of its crude
iron; and in thus lowering the price of ore there may have

---

[1] *Report of the Industrial Commission*, vol. xiii, pp. 471, 472.

been an element of reciprocity. It has been, however, the purpose of the corporation and other steel concerns owning their own ore fields to keep the price of ore high.   This policy is due to the desire to raise the cost of production for rival steel mills not owning, or owning very little, ore property.   In 1903 the price of Bessemer ore was $4.50 per ton.[1]   The Merchant's Ore Association wished to make the price for 1904 between $3.25 and $3.80, while the Steel Corporation demanded that $4.00 be made the price, threatening to sell ore itself.   In wishing to make the lower price the Ore Association was actuated by a desire to sell the largest possible amount of product.   The price was ultimately fixed at $3.50, although several of the members of the Association made long-term contracts to deliver at a sliding scale price fluctuating with the price of pig iron.[2] In this instance the influence of the Steel Corporation did not prevail; but its attempt to hold up the price of ore is typical of its general attitude toward the prices of raw products.

A somewhat similar attitude seems to be maintained toward the prices of crude and unfinished material.   The quotations, for example, of pig iron show greater fluctuations than those of finished products.   During the closing months of 1906 the prices of crude iron soared higher than they had ever done since 1899, whereas those of finished material did not in general reach the level of 1902.   Steel billets, out of which a variety of finished commodities are manufactured, and among them steel rails, were quoted at $32.00 per ton in June, 1902, and at $29.50 during the closing months of 1906 and the opening months of 1907. During both these prosperous periods, however, the price of steel rails remained fixed at $28.00.

[1] *Journal of Commerce*, New York, Apr. 22, 1904.
[2] *Iron Age*, May 5, 1904.

These instances, and others which might be cited, indicate a conservative policy with regard to the sales of finished material and a disposition not to discourage any "leveling up" of the prices of raw and crude products. By pursuing this business policy, steel makers discourage competition from the outside; and the steel industry tends to be confined to those already in the field and owning their own sources of raw material. Prosperity, therefore, brings little inducement to outsiders to enter the steel trade. This policy has given rise to much criticism on the part of independent producers; [1] but it has saved the consumer from paying very high prices for goods during those times when he needed them most.

§ 7. A comparison of the prices during the present boom and those of 1901 and 1902 further illustrates the tendency toward moderation in the case of finished commodities. The fall and winter months of 1906 and 1907 mark the most prosperous period in the history of the iron and steel trade and the highest levels reached by prices since 1902. The highest quotations during these two periods for certain standard products are as follows:

	1901-1903.	*Sept. 1906 to Feb. 1907.*
Foundry pig iron, No. 2, Philadelphia, per ton.	$23.00	$26.50
Bessemer pig iron, Pittsburg, per ton.	21.75	23.85
Steel billets, Pittsburg, per ton....	32.50	29.50
Wire rods, Pittsburg, per ton......	39.00	37.00
Bar iron, Pittsburg, per 100 lbs.....	1.80	1.80
Tank plate, Pittsburg, per 100 lbs.	1.85	1.70
Wire nails, Pittsburg, per 100 lbs.	2.30	2.00

With the exception of foundry and Bessemer pig iron, the prices of these materials were either lower or not higher during the later boom than during the earlier one. This

[1] *Evening Post*, New York, Dec. 31, 1906.

is worthy of note as the volume of trade for 1906 was greater throughout the world than in any previous year.

§ 8. It is seen therefore that one marked effect which the Steel Corporation has had on prices has been to render them more steady. It has been compelled to meet considerable competition; and it has been driven to a policy of moderation' during times of prosperity in order to save itself from the results of a cutthroat rivalry in periods of depression. More than any other steel company the United States Steel Corporation must maintain a large volume of business without interruption in order to meet heavy charges. Controlling as it does over half the steel trade of the country, it has been able during periods of prosperity to check the number of rivals entering the trade by keeping prices from rising abnormally high. By this policy competition is rendered less severe in times of depression.

A further consideration in this purpose of the corporation is the steadying of trade. While it is true that fluctuations in prices are due to fluctuations in demand, it is also true that prices react on demand. It is well known, for example, that on a declining market the consumer is tempted to wait for prices to get lower. He is furthermore inspired with fear concerning the future; and delayed demand results in a depression more or less prolonged. Oscillations in prices therefore have their psychological effect which is shown to some extent in the vicissitudes of trade. No explanation of such a phenomenon as a commercial panic is adequate without due consideration of this psychological element. In reducing the fluctuations of prices we may thus look forward to an appreciable steadying of the volume of trade. Not that variations in demand will be done away with, but that the more extreme phases of these oscillations will be considerably reduced.

The economy of steady as opposed to varying production has been indicated in a previous chapter.[1] With the same amount of trade more is wasted in meeting a fluctuating demand than in satisfying a steady and moderately strong demand. The shutting down and opening up of mills and furnaces involves a consumption of energy which in a technical sense is unproductive. The attempt, moreover, to curtail expenses in times of depression by lowering wages generally meets with more or less opposition from workmen, which not unfrequently results in strikes and lockouts. To reduce these and other wastes is itself a powerful motive in the effort to steady trade.

§ 9. A subject which has received considerable public attention in recent years is the prices charged by the Steel Corporation and other companies in the foreign market. This question has arisen in connection with investigations concerning the influence of the tariff on home prices and certain allegations that foreign consumers are favored at the expense of domestic purchasers. In 1901, after the Steel Corporation had been organized, steel rails were quoted at $28.00 per ton for the domestic consumer and delivered to the European buyer at $23.00.[2] Plain wire during the same period was quoted to the Canadian dealer at $11.00 per ton less than to the home dealer. It is reported that Mr. Schwab informed Mr. Joseph Lawrence, M. P., that the Steel Corporation could deliver steel billets in England at $16.50 per ton.[3] The price of steel billets in the United States at the same time was $24.00. Such discriminating charges have naturally aroused public curiosity in regard to the reason why the domestic consumer should be compelled to pay more than the foreigner for the same goods.

[1] *Cf. supra,* ch. ii.

[2] *Report of the Industrial Commission,* vol. xiii, pp. 454, 464.

[3] *Report of the British Iron Trade Commission,* p. 123.

That these differences have existed at times is admitted by the officials of the Steel Corporation and other steel companies, but are defended on the ground that these lower prices brought no profit and represented only attempts to capture the foreign market.   It has been further urged that it is desirable to keep plants running at their full capacity; and when the home demand is not sufficient to do this, it is necessary to dispose of surplus product at relatively low prices abroad.   If the plants are not kept running to their full capacity, it is contended that the cost of production would be so much increased that the price to the home consumer would on the whole be higher than if the export goods were sold at the lower rate.[1]   Whatever may be thought of the validity of these contentions, it is true that goods are often sold in foreign or distant markets at, or even below, cost in order to capture trade.   The price of $16.50 per ton for steel billets delivered in England, reported to have been named by Mr. Schwab, was probably not above the cost of manufacture to the Steel Corporation. In 1894 the Bethlehem Steel Company entered into a contract with the Russian government for the sale of armor plate which was much below the price charged to this government.   The action was defended on the ground that the price was below cost and entered into solely to secure trade. Recent investigations by a board appointed by the Secretary of the Navy have shown the justice of the defense;[2] and later contracts with Russia by this and the Carnegie Company at prices of one hundred to one hundred and fifty dollars more per ton of armor plate than the previous price charged have justified the policy as a matter of business.

During prosperous periods when the demand at home is

[1] *Report of the Industrial Commission,* vol. xiii, pp. 454, 455, 464.
[2] *Iron Age,* Dec. 13, 1906, p. 1604.

strong, it is usually affirmed by steel producers that the prices which they charge in the United States are no higher than those which they charge abroad. That the Steel Corporation to-day is selling at lower prices in Europe, Canada, and Mexico than at home is emphatically denied. This denial seems to be confirmed in the case of steel rails in Europe by the export prices fixed by the International Rail Syndicate. This organization was formed in 1904 of the leading steel rail producers of Germany, England, France and Belgium. When the syndicate was first formed it put the export price of rails at £4-5s to £4-10s per ton at port of shipment. Lately, however, the price has been fixed at £5-15s to £6. From these figures it is seen that steel rails are selling as high in Europe to-day as in the United States, while the cost of production is probably lower than here.

§ 10. Connected with the subject of domestic and export prices is the much discussed case concerning the charges made to the home and foreign governments for the sale of armor plate. Allusion has already been made to the contract entered into in 1904 by the Bethlehem Steel Company for the sale of 1500 tons of armor plate to the Russian government at a price much below that charged to this government. Last spring a special board appointed pursuant to an act of Congress made an investigation of the prices charged to this and other governments for armor plate and its actual cost of production. The following table as given in the report of the board shows the prices paid by the leading countries of the world for all types of armor and the maximum price paid for Krupp armor: [1]

---

[1] *Iron Age*, Dec. 13, 1906, p. 1604.

	Average price of all armor.	*Price of Krupp armor.*
Japan.....................per ton	$400.00	per ton $400.00
Austria................. " "	449.00	" " 557.00
Italy.................... " "	521.00	" " 550.00
Germany................ " "	450.00	" " 450.00
France .... " "	569.00	" " 572.00
England................ " "	626.00	" " 681.00
United States............ " "	345.00	" " 346.00

From the board's investigations it appears that the manufacturers of this country are practically alone in demanding of the home government no greater and even lower prices for armor than those charged to foreign customers. Very generally abroad home prices rule higher than those to foreign purchasers.

There are three armor-plate mills in the United States—the Carnegie, the Bethlehem, and the Midvale. Of these the Carnegie mill is the largest. The board made a careful investigation of the cost of producing armor plate at all three places and then divided its estimated costs into two kinds: production cost, and full cost. The former includes the price of all raw material, cost of labor, cost of up-keep of plant, the current repairs, salaries of superintendents, and interest on capital. Full cost includes in addition taxes, insurance, and a host of other expenses which cannot be readily itemized. The board estimated that the cost of armor plate of grade A (armor five inches or more in thickness) would be $244.27 per ton, production cost, and $296.89 per ton, full cost. Armor plate of grade B (armor less than five inches in thickness) costs $221.76, production cost, and $273.78, full cost. The board emphasizes the fact that cost depends largely on output. Working to the full capacity is the most economical.

In general it may be said concerning domestic and export prices that producers in all countries have endeavored to secure foreign trade and have often lowered prices to the foreign consumer to attain this end.   In dull years so-called surplus product has been disposed of in foreign markets in order to keep prices relatively high at home.   A high protective tariff, by shutting out foreign products, has enabled the producers of such countries as the United States and Germany to keep prices high in the home country while selling to foreigners at very low rates.   For reasons which will be indicated in the following chapter this practice seems likely to disappear in the future.

In reference to the attitude of steel companies to the government, particularly in the matter of armor plate, there seems to be no reason to believe that the American producers have made a practice of favoring the foreign purchaser. Certain indications, however, point to the Carnegie and Bethlehem companies having combined to raise the charges made to the United States government.   In December, 1903, when a contract was made with the Midvale company for 6080 tons of armor of class A for the American navy at $398.00 per ton, the Carnegie and Bethlehem companies both put in a bid at $420.00.   Again in April, 1905, when a second proposal for armor plate was made, the bids of the Carnegie and Bethlehem companies were the same—$400 to $420 per ton, while those of the Midvale company were from $385 to $398.   A recent contract has awarded the making of armor plate to all three companies notwithstanding the higher bids of the Carnegie and Bethlehem companies.   This rather strange award was made on the threat that the mills of the latter companies would be dismantled, leaving the Midvale establishment the only one in the United States manufacturing armor plate.   Whatever in general may be said of the relations existing between these organizations and the United States Government, their charges seem to compare very favorably with those made by foreign manufacturers to their own home governments.

The practice of demanding more of the home government than of foreign purchasers has probably been greatest in those nations where it has been least denounced.

§ 11. The influence which the Steel Corporation is likely to exert upon the general level of prices will depend in part upon the preservation of competitive conditions. Aside from the increasing control which it is securing in the Lake Superior region, there is no evidence of any drift toward monopoly conditions. There is very little reason to believe that it is able by virtue of mere size to manufacture more cheaply than its best equipped competitors. It has, however, certain advantages in the location of mines and in transportation facilities, which in the lower stages of production greatly cheapen cost. The Steel Corporation owns its own means of transportation from the ore mines of Minnesota and Michigan to the furnaces of Pennsylvania and Ohio. On its leased properties it has paid royalties of fifteen to thirty-five cents per ton for some of its best ores. These rates are cheaper than those charged for most of the ore mined by its competitors. By its superior transportation facilities and low royalties on ore the cost of this material to the Steel Corporation at its blast furnaces in Pennsylvania and Ohio has been on the average from seventy-five cents to a dollar and a half cheaper per ton than for independent companies.

These advantages, however, are likely to be neutralized in part by the higher royalties which the corporation will be obliged to pay for recent additions to its ore properties. As has been seen in a former chapter, the acquisition of the Hill holdings will cost the corporation $1.65 per ton for ore mined during the year 1907 with an increase of 3.4 cents per ton for each succeeding year.[1] The minimum

[1] *Iron Age*, Oct. 11, 1906, p. 953.

agreed to be mined is 750,000 tons for 1907 and thereafter 750,000 tons additional for each succeeding year until the output reaches 8,250,000 tons. What the cost to the Steel Corporation will be if the minimum tonnage is mined each year until 1917 is seen in the following table:

Year.	Minimum tonnage.	Price per ton.	Cost to the Steel Corporation.
1907	750,000	$1.650	$1,237,500
1908	1,500,000	1.684	2,526,000
1909	2,250,000	1.718	3,865,000
1910	3,000,000	1.752	5,256,000
1911	3,750,000	1.786	6,697,500
1912	4,500,000	1.820	8,190,000
1913	5,250,000	1.854	9,733,500
1914	6,000,000	1.888	11,328,000
1915	6,750,000	1.922	12,973,000
1916	7,500,000	1.956	14,670,000
1917	8,250,000	1.990	16,417,500

The price of the ore given in the above table is that for the standard based on 59 per cent iron contents. The royalty is reduced as the quality falls below the standard in proportion to iron contents. Below 48 per cent the royalty will be a matter for future negotiation, with recourse to arbitration.

The Steel Corporation, therefore, will pay the Great Northern a high price for taking all the ore it has to offer. While this transaction has greatly increased the holdings of the corporation, it will add much as years go on to the previous cost of supplying raw material. The marking-up of ore values will doubtless improve the position of independent producers already owning their sources of raw material. The increasing value of mining properties, however, and the policy of the Steel Corporation in keeping down the prices of finished products in prosperous times will make it harder for the outsider to enter the field and for the companies not controling their supplies of ore to maintain their position.

§ 12. In general, it may be said that the most obvious influence of the Steel Corporation on market conditions has been in the direction of steadying, rather than raising prices. One of its objects has been to lessen the fluctuations of the iron and steel trade; and this purpose it has striven to accomplish by making prices relatively uniform. It has been enabled to exercise this influence through its large share of the country's trade. The Steel Corporation in attempting to steady prices has recognized the wastefulness of intermittent production. Its general policy from a business man's standpoint has been a conservative one. Its stand for reasonable prices in times of great demand helps to check the number of competitors who would otherwise enter the field; and this policy operates to prevent cutthroat competition in a period of depression. Since its organization the general level of prices do not seem to have been above what market conditions would justify. In attempting to influence prices its power has been limited by the fact that it does not control the productive forces of the iron and steel industry. The means by which this control may be secured will be considered in the following chapter.

CHAPTER VII

Monopoly and Iron Associations

§ 1. In the formation of the United States Steel Corporation, industrial centralization reached a climax. The capital of this company far exceeded that of any other industrial organization in the world. Notwithstanding its commanding position among combinations, it has not, as we have seen, secured control of the country's output of iron and steel. It exercises no such influence over the manufacture of iron and steel goods as does the Standard Oil Company, for example, over the refining and distribution of oil. During the six years of its existence it has produced less than forty-five per cent of the country's ore and pig iron, and has manufactured less than sixty-five per cent of its steel ingots. Of rolled and finished material—excluding wire nails and tin plate,—it has controlled the output of less than half. Of wire nails and tin plate the corporation has manufactured between sixty-five and seventy-five per cent.

The corporation's share of the country's trade cannot, therefore, be said to constitute it a monopoly. In every consolidation, however, there inheres some element of monopoly. A great combination is organized primarily to regulate or restrict competition; and this, as has been shown in an earlier chapter, was the immediate cause which gave birth to the Steel Corporation. The object of such a consolidation is not so much a better adaptation to market conditions, as control of those conditions. In so far as this latter end has been attained, a combination may be said to have reached the position of a monopoly.

§ 2. Monopoly results from one or more of the following conditions: creation by law; ownership or possession of the sources of raw material; control of transportation; or ownership of trade-marks or brands which have secured great popular favor. To these may be added certain means by which competition is restricted or throttled by concerns which have already secured a large share of the country's trade. These means have been carefully discussed by Professor Clark in his *Problem of Monopoly*. They are factors' agreements, local underselling, and the underselling of one or a few lines of goods by a company engaged in trading in a large number of products. A combination of all the firms or companies of a country engaged in an industry will also, of course, produce a monopoly; but the control of trade established by such a combination is likely to be of short duration unless supported by one or more of the conditions which have just been given.

The old form of legal monopoly by which a particular trade was guaranteed to a certain concern in return for a stipulated tax has virtually disappeared. At the present time the chief monopolies created by law are in the form of patent rights and local franchises. The former and generally the latter are limited as to time; and their creation is due to real or supposed public benefits to be derived from such grants. A local franchise is not always intended to give a concern complete control of local trade or traffic; but in such cases as gas, telephone, and street-car companies, it often does this.

The possession of the sources of raw material enables a concern to control in large measure the production, and therefore the prices, of goods dependent upon those sources. This possession in the case of most commodities is difficult to secure.   Monopolies due to this condition are rare in this country, and confined almost entirely to mining products.

The control of transportation has been an effective means of building up and maintaining organizations monopolistic in nature.   By the phrase, control of transportation, is here meant not only the possession of a means of conveyance not enjoyed by others, as in the case of the Standard Oil Company and its pipe line system, but also railroad favoritism, by which a large corporation secures certain transportation rates and facilities not granted to smaller rivals.   This control in the United States has generally taken the form of railroad discriminations in favor of certain large shippers.   In putting small or competing concerns at a disadvantage, this condition has been a potent influence in the development of monopoly.

The influence of favorite brands and trade-marks is psychological in its nature.   Clever advertising induces people to demand certain brands or trade-marks; and the exclusive possession of these gives the holder a great advantage over rivals producing commodities equally good, and enables him to exact monopoly prices.   Such an advantage is due to the mental attitude of the buyer.   Take away his prejudices and the monopoly is gone.

The other means by which monopoly power is secured and competition is restricted or repressed are means which can generally be resorted to only by organizations which have already built up a very large trade.   Factors' agreements are used to secure and conserve for a consolidation or trust the exclusive trade of a wholesale or retail establishment.   Such contracts help to confine trade to the articles manufactured by the trust.   The agreements between the American Sugar Refining Company and the Wholesale Grocers' Association, the American Tobacco Company and the concerns selling its products, seem to be of this nature.

Local underselling and the underselling of a particular line of goods have been used by large producers to crush local competition or competition in a particular branch of manufacture. Where a large producer meets competition in a certain locality the goods of the large concern are sold within that area at a price below the cost of production and ruinous to the rival firm. Losses which the larger organization suffers are made good by high prices in other places. In like manner competition in a single line or grade of goods is crushed by lowering prices below cost in that particular line or grade, and recouping losses by high prices on other goods.

§ 3. Comparing these conditions of monopoly growth and conservation with the conditions obtaining in the iron and steel industry, it may be observed that the Steel Corporation from the nature of its trade is not likely to resort to certain of these means in order to secure a monopoly control. The purchasers of steel rails and steel plate, for example, are not as a rule affected by those prejudices which enable the manufacturers of other commodities to create an artificial demand for particular brands and trademarks. These devices, so potent in many industries, would have little influence in enlarging the control exercised by the corporation over the iron and steel trade. Nor are factors' agreements likely to play any important rôle in promoting monopoly, as a large proportion of the goods manufactured by the steel consolidation is sold directly to customers. Local underselling cannot be employed as a means for crushing competition because the strongest independent companies sell their commodities to more than local areas. The selling below cost of a single line of goods in order to ruin a rival concern is not likely to be extensively resorted to in view of the fact that the strongest competitors of the corporation are engaged in several branches of manufacture. This practice has been indulged in by iron and steel concerns in the past, and rumors are not wanting that it has been employed in recent times. When the Carnegie and Bethlehem companies were underbid by the Midvale Steel Company in the sale of armor plate to the United States government, it was rumored that these concerns threatened " to slash prices " and destroy the armor plate trade of the Midvale Company.[1] The threat, however, if made, was not carried out. For the reason already given this practice is not likely to be employed by the Steel Corporation to destroy competition.

The Steel Corporation has enjoyed a monopoly in certain lines of wire goods by virtue of patent rights.[2] This monopoly, however, has covered but a small proportion of the company's trade, and could contribute but little to its dominance in the iron and steel industry.

The possible control of transportation by the Steel Corporation demands some attention. The corporation owns most of the railroad and steamship lines over which its ores are carried from the mines of Minnesota and Michigan to the furnaces of Ohio and Pennsylvania. No independent company has as complete facilities for assembling its raw material as has this organization. By means of this control the cost of ore to the corporation at its blast furnaces in Ohio and Pennsylvania is from seventy-five cents to one dollar and a half cheaper per ton than for its competitors. This control, however, is limited to facilities for the assembling of ore and coal.

In regard to the shipment of commodities from plant to market or to consumer, the corporation enjoys no special advantage over independent companies. Whether or not

[1] *The Times*, New York, Dec. 27, 1904.

[2] See *First Annual Report*.

it has to any appreciable extent received favors from railroads is difficult to determine. In December, 1905, an indictment was returned by the Federal Grand Jury in Chicago against the Chicago, Burlington and Quincy Railroad,
the first vice-president of the road, and its foreign freight
agent for having granted rebates to the United States Steel
Products Export Company of New York, the company
under whose management the export trade of the Steel
Corporation is carried on. In this indictment twenty-six
offences were charged. It was alleged in the indictment that
the rebates amounted to about thirty per cent of the sched-
uled tariff. Under this charge the defendants were found
guilty and fined. It is worthy of note, however, notwithstanding this rather flagrant case, that early in the corporation's history independent organizations seem to have felt
little concern about their ability to compete with the new
company;[1] and at the present time the fear of railroad
discrimination does not prevail to any considerable extent
among the corporation's competitors. The attitude, moreover, of some of the leading officials of the corporation has
been friendly toward those measures of Federal regulation
which are calculated to do away with railroad favoritism.[2]
The increasing stringency of legislation against railroad
discrimination will make the rebate a less potent factor in
promoting the growth of monopoly in the future than it has
been in the past.

§ 4. If the Steel Corporation obtains control of the country's output of iron and steel, it is likely to do so by securing
possession of the principal deposits of ore in the United

---

[1] *Report of the Industrial Commission,* vol. xiii; see testimonies of
King *et al.*

[2] See remarks of Judge Gary on Federal regulation, New York *World,*
Mar. 24, 1907.

States. The control of the nation's ore supply will not be easy to secure owing to the great extent of deposits. Nevertheless, the corporation has been increasing its holdings in the Lake Superior region to such an extent that it may now be said to control the output of that district. Just what proportion of the ore of this region is now held by the Steel Corporation cannot be stated very definitely, but it is probably not much less than eighty per cent. When it is remembered that this northern field probably contains over half the visible supply of workable ore in the country, the significance of the large holdings of the corporation can be readily appreciated. As a result of recent additions to its properties the company's share of the country's output of ore will probably increase, and it is not unlikely that further efforts will be made to secure ore lands in other parts of the country. The annual report for 1906, just recently issued, after speaking of the large additions made to its properties by the transfer of the Hill holdings, says very significantly : " It is, however, doubtful if the quantity of new ore so obtained will prove sufficient to meet the constantly-increasing demands upon the ore reserves made by the country's growing requirements for steel products."

It has already been observed that for much of the production of this district a high royalty must be paid. In the case of the Great Northern properties recently transferred to the corporation this royalty for standard ore (59 per cent iron contents) delivered at shipping port on Lake Superior will be, as we have seen, $1.65 per ton in 1907 (85 cents royalty plus 80 cents haulage), with an increase each year of $.034, which royalty is to apply to a minimum tonnage increasing each year until 1917, when the annual production is to be at least 8,250,000 tons. The price paid by the Carnegie Company for its ore holdings before the Steel Corporation was organized ranged from fifteen to thirty-five cents per ton for standard grade. It will thus be seen that high-grade ore is commanding a much higher royalty now than in the closing years óf the last century.

The whole transaction seems to have been based on the belief that the bulk of the iron ore in the United States that can be carried at reasonable freight rates to advantageous assembling points for fuel and ore is known to-day, and that if other ore deposits are found they will be at such distances from the chief steel-making and steel-consuming sections of the country as not to compete on equal terms with the Lake ores. It seems to be based also on the conviction that the demand for iron and steel will continue to increase, and consequently that the high price paid for the late additions to the corporation's holdings is reasonable, if not low, in comparison with future values.

That the demand for iron and steel is pressing hard upon the ore supply of the country seems to be indicated by the general trend of prices during the last six or eight years. In the spring of 1900 Old Range Bessemer ore sold as low as $2.75 per ton at furnace. This price was lower than for 1899, when all iron and steel goods sold at unusually high figures. It was not, however, considered very low. Four years later the price of Old Range Bessemer ore was $3.25 per ton, which was considered almost ruinous. In the fall of 1906 it was $5.15.[1] Non-Bessemer Mesaba ore, which sold for $2.75 per ton at furnace in 1901, sold at the latter date for $4.10.[2] These prices indicate that there has been a marking up of ore values during recent years. The high price paid by the Steel Corporation for the Hill holdings is but a recognition of the general trend of values.

The Steel Corporation is thus in possession of large areas of ore land which are steadily increasing in value. It is

---

[1] *Iron Trade Review*, Feb. 28, 1907.   [2] *Ibid.*

furthermore in control of the district from which nearly all the Bessemer ore of the United States comes, and may therefore be said virtually to control the output of this material. It is well known that Bessemer ore is getting scarcer the world over. The Bilbao district of Spain, which has supplied Europe with a large proportion of this material, will, according to all accounts, soon be exhausted. The large ore fields of Asturias, which are not yet fully opened up, will not produce ores suitable for the acid Bessemer process. The Bessemer ore of Lake Superior is not likely, therefore, to experience much foreign competition. In this country Bessemer ore still commands a higher price than the non-Bessemer product. As long as this is the case the control of the Lake Superior region will give the Steel Corporation a marked advantage over its competitors.

It has been pointed out, however, in a former chapter that the open-hearth process is gaining favor with manufacturers and seems to be displacing the Bessemer mode of production. This fact has been recognized by the Steel Corporation itself; and most of its new plants have been equipped for the open-hearth process of steel manufacture. The new rail mills to be built at Gary, Indiana, will manufacture rails from open-hearth steel. The introduction of the basic mode of producing steel, both in the form used in Germany and England, and in the form used in this country in connection with the open-hearth process, has already destroyed the monopoly once enjoyed by Bessemer steel. Notwithstanding the fact that this latter product is still preferred to other kinds of steel, the growing demand for the open-hearth material seems calculated to neutralize whatever advantage Bessemer steel may now possess.

While the Steel Corporation now holds the most valuable ore fields in the United States and has certain advantages in its control of the output of Bessemer ore, it is meeting increasing competition. Its advance to virtual control of the Lake Superior region, especially as marked in the Great Northern deal, has been signalized by increased activity in the South. Northern capital in increasing amounts is being invested in the iron industry of the South; and the Tennessee Coal, Iron and Railroad Company and the Southern Steel Company are increasing their holdings in the Alabama region. An extensive program of new construction has been laid out by the former company involving the expenditure of at least $7,000,000. " The Hill deal," says the *Iron Age,* " suggested to men of large capital that the psychological moment had arrived for investment in Alabama ore and coal, and in the plants already existing to turn them into steel." [1]

Competition from the South is thus likely to become more aggressive in the future. Up to the present time there has been little competition from this region, notwithstanding its great natural advantages. Its comparative remoteness from the great steel-consuming centers of the North and East has held back its development, and its production has been confined largely to iron materials. The general marking up of ore values shown in the Hill deal has given an impetus to the industry in this region; and present indications point to more intense rivalry with the steel producers of the North. It is in the interests of this region that the Steel Corporation is likely to meet its most formidable competitors in the future.

The Steel Corporation has an advantage over independent companies in possessing deposits of ore which will probably long outlast theirs. It dominates the Northern ore region; but its large possessions here do not enable it to control the country's output. In order to secure such a

[1] *Iron Age,* Nov. 22, 1906, pp. 1388, 1389.

control the corporation would, in addition to its present holdings in the Lake Superior district, have to gain possession of the Alabama region.

Rumors are not wanting that appraisals of the value of important iron and steel companies have been made with a view to an ultimate merger with the Steel Corporation.[1] Companies in possession of important ore fields would be the natural subjects of such appraisal. Were such organizations as the Republic Iron and Steel Company, the Tennessee Coal, Iron and Railroad Company, the Colorado Fuel and Iron Company, the Southern Steel Company, and the Sloss-Sheffield Company to be merged with the Steel Corporation on the basis of their present capitalization, something like $200,000,000 would be added to the stocks and bonds of the Corporation. A merger of this kind would by no means be so great as that which took place when the Steel Corporation itself was organized, and it would give the organization practically a control of the iron and steel trade of the country. Under such a combination the output of ore from Lake Superior, Alabama, Colorado and Utah would be regulated by one organization.

§ 5. The strength of a monopoly based upon control over the sources of raw material within the country would depend upon the protection given it by the tariff. Prices of iron and steel have until recently been lower in Europe than in the United States. The prices of finished material in bond at New York City are generally a few dollars per ton lower than those of the corresponding goods in this country. Ore and pig iron can also be imported at prices below those usually charged for the domestic product. The tariff would thus be an important factor in safeguarding any monopoly dependent upon control acquired over the sources

[1] *The Times*, New York, Mar. 6, 1906.

of raw material. In the present state of public opinion
with its intense feeling against anything savoring of monopoly the tariff protecting such a combination would be
the first object of attack.

§ 6. The United States Steel Corporation is not a monopoly. Whatever may be its developments in the direction
of ultimate control of the country's sources of ore supply, it
at present meets considerable domestic competition, and may
be compelled to meet not a little foreign rivalry. To say,
however, that no one consolidation controls the iron and
steel industry of the country is not to say that the situation
is not influenced by combinations of another character, and
that the Steel Corporation is not an influential force in such
combinations. As has already been indicated, prices have
often been agreed upon by pools or associations. Owing
to the hostile attitude of public opinion toward price agreements, and to the more rigid enforcement of the anti-trust
act, many of the old pools and associations have been form-
ally discontinued. Understandings in regard to prices,
however, persist, and the influence of former associations is
still a living force, and seems likely to continue so.

The full details of some of the best known pools are
difficult to ascertain. Most of these associations have come
to life and have died without attracting public attention.
Pooling agreements long preceded the era of great consolidations. The trust, or big corporation, which was intended
to do more effectually what the pool attempted to do, can
hardly be said to have supplanted that form of organization. In fact, pools or understandings in regard to prices
seemed to have been strengthened and extended simulta-
neously with the growth in size of our manufacturing companies. The growth of large consolidations by rendering
the number of producing organizations fewer has tended to
strengthen the pool. The recognition of the difficulties

involved in attempting to control the trade situation by means of a single corporate organization has also led to a revived interest in pools.

In the iron and steel industry there are certain funda- mental features common to nearly all forms of pooling. An unincorporated organization is formed by all manufac- turers of a certain class of commodities; and these agree to maintain a schedule of prices fixed by the association. In order to maintain these prices, production is limited according to the conditions of the market. Each manufac- turer is allowed to produce or sell only a specified percent- age of the total output—a percentage which is determined by the capacity and advantage of his plant. The agreement is often fortified by a money deposit, which is forfeitable to the association in case of violation. Where production is greater than the alloted percentage a fine is imposed; and a corresponding bonus given to plants producing less than their share in the allotment. Owing to the nature of the industry, territorial division of the market, which was a feature of railroad pools, has not been adopted. Prices, however, are made uniform by adopting a common base point, as Pittsburg for example, where the price would.be the factory price, and adding to this figure the freight rate to obtain the price at other points. In this case shipments from Pittsburg would increase in price, and toward it, would suffer loss.

The success of certain pools in the iron and steel industry has been mainly owing to the large capital now required to produce cheaply some of the most important commodi- ties, and the consequent small number of corporations which can engage in the industry on any considerable scale. It was noted in a previous chapter that the number of iron and steel establishments had declined during the last thirty years, notwithstanding the enormous increase of capital invested. The possession of sources of raw material which is now necessary to any organization expecting to compete with the largest steel corporations has also tended to limit the number of producers. In 1906 the number of steel companies capitalized at more than twenty million dollars was only about a dozen. The consolidations which entered the Steel Corporation had united into single corporations a great number of competing concerns. These concerns were then absorbed into a still larger combination. These conditions by limiting the number of independent plants have facilitated the formation of pools or associations of considerable strength. Those associations have been most powerful which have regulated the price of commodities produced by the fewest plants. Bessemer steel rails in the United States are produced by less than a dozen different plants, and the steel rail association is the strongest in the trade.

§ 7. The price of iron is regulated as soon as the ore is dug. The independent producers and sellers of ore have organized the Merchants' Ore Association of Cleveland. The United States Steel Corporation is not a seller of ore; but as it is a producer of this commodity, its influence is felt in the regulation of price. With the Steel Corporation the price is largely a matter of book-keeping. Nevertheless, its endeavor is to keep it high in order to raise the cost of production for rival mills not owning mines. As the Ore Association desires to sell the largest possible amount of product it has contended for low prices. This contention has led to compromises between the Steel Corporation and the Association, not very satisfactory to either party.[1]

This attitude of the Steel Corporation toward the price of ore is characteristic of its policy with regard to prices

[1] *Iron Age*, May 5, 1904.

of most crude material. This organization is, as we have seen, more disposed to favor high prices in prosperous times in the cases of ore, pig iron, steel billets, and the like, than in those of steel rails, steel beams, or steel plate. The object of this policy, as was indicated in the preceding chapter, is to limit the number of manufacturers of finished product by keeping up the cost of crude material.

§ 8. Pig iron and steel ingots have been the subject of price agreements. The attempt to pool steel-ingot production has been on the whole unsuccessful. The Bessemer Pig Iron Association is an organization of furnace men by which the price and production of pig iron are regulated. As in the cases of pools generally, allotments are made to different producers in percentages. The Association has had appreciable influence on prices; but the relatively increasing use of pig iron, not of Bessemer grade, has helped to limit this influence.

§ 9. The first steel billet pool was formed in April, 1896, as an attempt to reduce the great fluctuations in price which marked the year 1895.[1] The Bessemer Steel Association, as this pool was called, alloted the percentages in the usual manner, and imposed a fine of two dollars per ton for any excess produced. The selling price was fixed at $21.50 per ton. As this price was higher than was justified by the demand at this time, outside firms took orders at $19.50. Within the Association there was much selling contrary to the agreement, and the larger concerns, also, evaded the agreement by converting billets into finished shapes. The pool was therefore weak from the beginning and soon failed. Re-organization was attempted without much success.[2] In 1901, a sliding scale device was resorted to by which the price of steel billets was kept $6.50 above that of

[1] *Iron Age,* vol. i, p. 895; vol. ii, pp. 223, 967.   [2] *Ibid.,* Jan. 3, 1901.

pig iron.   This scale was adopted by the larger manufacturers; and the attempt to raise the price directly was not
made very seriously.   In July, 1903, an agreement was
entered into by certain companies by which the Pittsburg
price was fixed at $27.00 per ton.   Some of the prices at
other places were, $28.75 in New York, $28.00 in Chicago,
$40.25 in Pueblo, Colorado, and $39.25 in San Francisco.
The members of this pool were the United States Steel
Corporation, the Jones and Laughlin Company, the Wheeling Steel and Iron Company, the Cambria Steel Company,
the Pennsylvania Steel Company, the Lackawanna Steel
Company, and the Maryland Steel Company.[1]   This price
agreement, however, did not last.   In the depression of the
latter months of 1903 and of 1904 prices were cut.   In the
spring of 1904 the Pittsburg price had been reduced to
$23.00 per ton, and the prices at other places lowered cor-
respondingly.   The Billet Association has not been able to
control prices to any considerable degree.   The outside
supply has always been elastic, rendering billet manufacture
essentially competitive.

§ 10.   The strongest and best known pool in the iron industry is that of steel rails.   Organized in 1887,[2] it has
named prices, with a few interruptions in the nineties, for
nearly twenty years.   The original pool consisted of fifteen
members.   To each of these members was alloted a percentage of the total yield.   A penalty of $1.50 to $2.50 per
ton was imposed for all excesses beyond this allotment; and
thus the firms were kept from cutting prices in order to
secure more business.   The pool disbanded in February,
1897, and was not re-organized until 1899, from which
time dates the present pool.   At the time of the dissolution
of the old pool, in 1897, the members with their alloted per-

[1] *Iron Age,* July 23, 1903.   [2] *Ibid.,* Nov. 16, 1893.

centages were as follows: The Carnegie Company, 53.50; the Lackawanna, 19.00; the Cambria, 8.25; the Bethlehem, 8.25; the Pennsylvania, 8.25; and the Maryland, 2.75.[1]

Since the organization of the Steel Corporation, the Steel Rail Association has been able to maintain a uniform price for six years. This pool has probably had more permanent influence in naming prices than any other combination in the iron and steel trade. The most important member of this Association is, of course, the Steel Corporation, which is the main influence in shaping its policy. The attempt to fix the prices of rolled or finished products at moderately high figures and hold them there irrespective of the fluctuations of the trade, is an avowed purpose of the Steel Corporation; and this endeavor seems to have been most clearly realized in the case of steel rails. It must be said, however, that the price, $28.00 per ton, has not been much above what market conditions would seem to justify. In 1902, when the price of steel billets rose to $32.00 per ton, the Association kept the price of steel rails at $28.00, and therefore below what would then have probably been the price had conditions been strictly competitive. This moderation in times of prosperity enabled the Association to keep the price up during the depression of 1904. The fact that the Association has been obliged to exercise its power with moderation in order to prevent the rise of possible competitors shows that it is monopolistic in a very limited sense.

§ 11. The Steel Rail Association has excited considerable interest on account of its relations with the International Steel Rail Pool. In the fall of 1904 a meeting of the representatives of the leading rail-making concerns of Great Britain, Germany, Belgium and France was held in London.[2] The object of the meeting was to arrive at an under-

---

[1] *Iron Age*, Feb. 11, 1897, p. 18.   [2] *Ibid.*, Nov. 3, 1904, p. 45.

standing as to export orders, and prevent the ruinous cutting of prices that had hitherto taken place in this industry. A provisional arrangement was entered into by which the four countries named were to export 1,300,000 tons per annum for three years in the following proportions:[1]

British works....................................	53.50
German works....................................	28.83
Belgium works....................................	17.67
	100.00

French works...First year....4.8 parts out of 104.8 parts.
Second year..5.8 parts out of 105.8 parts.
Third year...6.4 parts out of 106.4 parts.

It will be seen that the allotments are based upon proportions of 104.8, 105.8 and 106.4 parts for the three years, and that the share of France increases slightly from year to year. This agreement was subject to the approval of the works of the countries interested.

In the summer of 1905 it was "known in trade circles that the leading steel rail manufacturers in this country and Europe have been working together quite closely."[2] Details of an arrangement were published whereby it was stated that the American manufacturers were to be given the steel rail trade of the American continent, and that European manufacturers were to be free from American competition in all parts of the world except South Africa. The English and French works were to have the prior right of furnishing rails to their colonies, while German works were to have the prior right in Norway, Sweden and Denmark. Other international trade was divided among English, German, Belgium and French establishments.

How far these arrangements are being seriously carried

[1] *Iron Age,* Nov. 3, 1904, p. 45.   [2] *Ibid.,* July 6, 1905, p. 22.

out it is difficult at present to say.   Assuming the announcements to be true, some interesting points suggest themselves.   If European competition for steel rail orders in this country is removed by such an international pool, the reduction or even complete abolition of the tariff on steel rails would not serve to lower prices.   Assuming that the agreement is adhered to, such a pool would be even more effective in limiting the area of competition than a high tariff itself.   This assumption is, of course, extravagant, as pools are notoriously weak in dull times; and an international association would probably be less effective than a national one.

Another result likely to follow the formation of such a pool is that countries producing no rails would have to pay higher prices than they now do.   Under existing conditions it is the producing countries which are generally protected by tariff regulations, and within which high prices are charged.   Countries not producing steel rails are generally open to the widest competition; and prices are often at cost, and not infrequently below cost.   An international pool guaranteeing certain territories to the manufacturing interests of particular nations would enable national pools so to operate as to reduce the necessity of cutting the prices of exported commodities in order to secure foreign trade.   Such an outcome cannot be said to be undesirable.   It is indeed an anomaly that a country producing steel rails should have to pay several dollars per ton more than a country not manufacturing such a product situated thousands of miles away.   Such a condition is a contravention of the natural laws of trade.   If the rail buyer in South America, South Africa or Arabia should be compelled to pay the going price in the United States, England or Germany, plus freight to destination, he would not be treated unfairly.   Nor will the home consumer be making extreme

demands in expecting some of the consideration which producing concerns have shown themselves able to accord to
foreign consumers.

It is yet too early to measure the probable outcome of
the movement in the direction of international pooling.
The great area covered and the number of establishments
included would tend to make an international pool exceedingly difficult to maintain.   The complexity of the legal
and political situation under which the pool would have to
operate would certainly enhance this difficulty.   Industrial
combinations, however, have shown a disposition in late
years to overstep national boundaries; and it is not unlikely
that this disposition will show itself in several of the·more
important lines of the iron and steel trade.

§ 12. The Rail Association is the strongest combination
of its kind in the iron and steel industry. While it has
been compelled to act with moderation, it has been able to
hold prices at a fairly high level.   This strength and moderation have also been shown by the beam pool, which, next
to the Rail Association, seems to be the most firmly established pool in the trade.   It was organized late in the
eighties; and like other organizations of a similar character
at first set prices far above what market conditions would
justify.   After some breaks, the present pool was formed
in 1898 by six leading firms. These firms were the Carnegie
Steel Company, Jones and Laughlin Company, the Cambria
Steel Company, the Pennsylvania Steel Company, the Pas-
saic Iron Works, and the Pencoyd Iron Works.[1]   In 1899,
when billet prices rose, the beam manufacturers advanced
prices by leaps and bounds. With the depression of 1900
prices fell. After the organization of the Steel Corporation the price of beams was fixed at $1.60 per hundred

[1] *Iron Age*, Jan. 12, 1902.

pounds, Pittsburg, and kept there. During the prosperous year of 1902 the steadiness of the price of steel beams was in marked contrast with the fluctuations of 1899. This change of policy on the part of the pool was certainly due to the influence of the Steel Corporation.

§ 13. Some other associations, like that of the steel plate pool, have shown considerable strength. In general, however, these associations while numerous seem to show great stability only when the number of producers to be combined is small. Even then their power must be characterized by moderation. The influence of the Steel Corporation seems to have been directed towards this end. This conservative policy has probably been due to a realization of the essentially unstable character of a pool.

In Germany a similar disposition toward moderation in prices is noted by Professor Jenks in the case of the great coal combination of Westphalia. During the late nineties when the demand for coal exceeded all previous demands, prices remained uniform. It was claimed by the syndicate that moderate prices in good times prevented low prices in periods of depression. In the steel trade of the same country a like tendency is noticeable. During the prosperous months of the summer of 1906 the German Verband refused to advance the price of billets, sheet-bars, slabs, skelp, and other half-rolled material five per cent.[1] The career of this combination shows that its attempt has been to steady rather than to raise prices. The influence of the German government has probably been responsible in part for this moderation. Aside from this governmental influence, however, the effect of abnormally high prices seems everywhere to be disastrous to the permanent business welfare of any combination.

[1] *Iron Age*, Aug. 16, 1906, p. 418.

That the general level of prices is higher than would have been the case if pools or mutual understandings in regard to prices did not exist is probably true.   These organizations have had an appreciable influence on market conditions.   The persistence of competition, however, reduces this power to comparatively narrow limits.   A writer in the *Iron Age* says:

It is very doubtful if an agreement as to prices has ever been faithfully kept.   While the established price in one particular product may, to all intents and purposes, be faithfully kept, concessions are made on closely allied manufactures in the buyer's favor.   In the closing months of the nail pool, while the established price of $2.55 on wire nails was probably kept, prices of smooth and barb wire were cut to ridiculous figures in order to stimulate sales of nails.[1]

Even in the case of the rail pool the maintenance of the agreed price has gone hand in hand with great reductions in the prices of allied material.   During the depression of 1904, rail makers while adhering to the pool agreement made concessions to the buyers of steel rails in the shape of low prices on angle bars, bolts, and spikes.[2]

In the case of crude material, pools are often rendered inoperative for other reasons.   The number of producers is relatively large, and pools are therefore more difficult to maintain.   The temptation, too, on the part of the members to evade agreements by converting crude into finished material is also great.   It has been the yielding to this temptation which has weakened all pools for the control of billet and ingot prices.   On the whole, the influence of pools on prices in general seems much less than is generally sup-

[1] *Iron Age*, Jan. 7, 1897, p. 12.
[2] *Ibid.*, Jan. 5, 1905, p. 82.

posed.   For short periods of time, and in particular lines, their influence may be great.   Their power, however, to exert a permanent control over market conditions seems at present rather limited.

§ 14. The laws with respect to pooling are not entirely satisfactory.   If all the anti-trust laws on the statute books were enforced, thousands of members and hundreds of officers of these associations would be defendants in civil or criminal suits.   Yet pools are as numerous as ever.   This condition is not a healthy one, as obedience to the law is a cardinal prerequisite to good citizenship.   It is not possible by law to prevent all price agreements, nor is it advisable to attempt it.   In an industry like that of iron and steel, subject to great fluctuations of trade, the high prices of prosperous times afford a powerful inducement to enter the field on the part of outsiders, who in periods of depression must themselves be driven out, or drive out older producers.   Such a condition is conducive to great waste. Manufacturers would seem to be justified in making some agreement to protect themselves, and to prevent wasteful industrial warfare.   It would seem that some statutes might be devised enabling manufacturers to co-operate for self-protection, and at the same time prohibiting the formation of conspiracies to exact tribute.

CONCLUSION

In the light of what has been said in the preceding pages some mention may be made of the Steel Corporation in its relations to the trust movement in general. During the last eight or ten years this movement has bulked large in the industrial affairs of the United States. The apparent success of several of the larger combinations has led some of the ablest business men and economists to the conclusion that the trust has become an established factor in the industrial life of the nation, and that trusts are economically beneficial. Some, however, have vigorously disputed this conclusion, and have contended that the larger business combinations have grown and maintained their ascendency, not by superior efficiency as producers, but by the employment of means giving them advantages monopolistic in nature over independent concerns.

How far the alleged economies of consolidation really lower their cost of production and improve their competitive efficiency depends in large part upon the industry in which the combination is formed. It has been noted that the iron and steel industry is characterized by conditions which make large-scale production economical. Though this condition has tended to limit the number of producers to a relatively few large companies, it is doubtful if the competitive strength of such a combination as the Steel Corporation is greater by virtue of mere size than that of some of the more important independent companies with only a fraction of its capital. The reports of the American

Iron and Steel Association certainly do not show that the larger organization is gaining on its smaller rivals in its share of the country's trade.   While " trusts are taken to mean manufacturing corporations with so great capital and power that they are at least thought by the public to have become a menace to their welfare and to have, temporarily at least, considerable monopolistic power," [1] it must be said that the Steel Corporation, the largest of the trusts, is meeting a considerable, and probably growing, competition.

Whatever question may be raised as to the efficiency of the trust as a producer, there is little reason to doubt its power to steady prices.   It has already been seen that one of the most potent factors working for consolidation in the iron and steel industry has been the violent fluctuation in the demand for goods resulting in great variations in prices. These price variations have been greatly reduced since the formation of the Steel Corporation.   While this organization has no monopoly control over market conditions, it has been enabled appreciably to steady market values by virtue of its large volume of trade, and has been impelled toward this policy by business considerations.   Such an influence can hardly be said to be prejudicial to public welfare.   The uncertainties and wastes due to alternating periods of prosperity and depression, while greater in the iron and steel industry than in most other lines of business, have been considerable in all departments of industrial activity.

An organization, however, whose trade is sufficiently large to influence market conditions will strive for a fuller and more monopolistic control over these conditions.   The advance of the Steel Corporation in the Lake Superior region seems indicative of a desire for ultimate possession

[1] J. W. Jenks, *The Trust Problem,* p. 8.

of the country's best sources of iron ore, and through this
for more absolute control of the steel trade. The possession of these deposits of ore will be difficult to secure; and
as we have seen, the influence which the Steel Corporation
is likely to wield over market conditions in the near future
will probably be in association with independent producers.

What effect monopoly power would have upon the policy
of the Steel Corporation is difficult to say. There is no
reason, however, to believe that it would have a radically
different effect upon this organization than upon any other.
As has been noted in the preceding pages, the business
policy of the company has thus far been characterized by
a judicious conservatism. Prices, as we have seen, have
not tended to increase. In the fifth annual report of the
corporation it is stated that the average prices received during the year 1906 for all steel products shipped to the
domestic trade exceeded by five and three-tenths per cent
the average received in 1905, but were eight per cent lower
than the prices which prevailed in 1902. This comparison
of the prices of 1906 with those of 1902 is significant.
These years were the two most prosperous years in the
history of the iron and steel industry of this country. In
1906 the price of ore was greater than in 1902; the wages
of labor were higher; freight rates had been raised; and
the demand for iron and steel was greater than in any
previous period. Notwithstanding all these conditions,
prices were eight per cent lower than in 1902. It is unlikely that such a showing would be made by an organization relieved from the pressure of actual or potential competition.

It should be noted in closing that the Steel Corporation
has set a worthy example to other combinations in its annual reports. These reports are issued to the stockholders,
and give with considerable detail the income and expendi-

tures of the organization.   Such an acknowledgment of the rights of stockholders to more detailed information concerning business operations than is usually supplied by large consolidations has inspired much public confidence in the corporation.   Recent exposures have shown the possible menace to public welfare in the secret and unqualified exercise of the power lodged in great capitalistic organizations. The publication by the company of a detailed report of its financial condition brings the policy of the consolidation into a wholesome accord with the growing demand for publicity of corporate accounts.

VITA

THE author of this thesis, Abraham Berglund, was born in San Francisco, California, December 10, 1875. He attended the public schools of that city, and prepared for college in the Boys' High School. He was graduated from the University of Chicago in 1904 with the degree of A. B., having already begun his graduate studies in economics, sociology, and history. In the year 1904-'05 he held a scholarship in Economics at Columbia University, in which institution he studied under Professors E. R. A. Seligman, John B. Clark, H. L. Moore, F. H. Giddings, John W. Burgess, and J. H. Robinson. During the year 1906-'07 he has been teaching in a college-preparatory school at Manlius, New York.